S0-AIN-193

Great Gardens of America

Great Gardens of America

GENERAL EDITOR:

CARROLL C. CALKINS

COWARD-McCANN, INC. and COUNTRY BEAUTIFUL
NEW YORK   WAUKESHA, WISCONSIN

Produced in association with Country Beautiful.

COUNTRY BEAUTIFUL: *Publisher and Editorial Director:* Michael P. Dineen; *Executive Editor:* Robert L. Polley; *Senior Editors:* Kenneth L. Schmitz, James H. Robb; *Associate Art Directors:* Wilbur Howe, Mitchel L. Heinrichs; *Photography:* Douglas C. Green; *Editorial Assistants:* Lawrence D. Kenney, Carolyn Muchhala; *Marketing Director:* Thomas R. Given; *Sales Manager:* James P. Green; *Executive Assistant:* Judy Hammond; *Circulation Manager:* Trudy Schnittka; *Production:* Michael Swan; *Editorial Secretary:* Donna Vincent; *Fulfillment:* Nola J. Cronick.

Frontispiece: Bellingrath, Mobile, Alabama

Copyright © 1969 by Country Beautiful. Library of Congress Catalogue Card Number 71-90381. All rights reserved. This book, or parts thereof, must not be reproduced in any form without permission. Published simultaneously in the Dominion of Canada by Longmans Canada Limited, Toronto. Manufactured in the United States of America. Book design by Wilbur Howe. Color separations, Mueller Color Plate Company.

CONTENTS

Introduction

On the pages that follow you will read about and see thirty-eight of the greatest gardens to be found in this abundant land of ours. They range in size from the Chance Gardens in Centralia, Missouri, complete in no more than an acre, to the grandeur of Callaway Gardens in Georgia with upwards of a thousand acres, including streams, lakes, woodlands and beautiful plantings. They are a fascinating cross section of a nation's interest in horticulture and garden design. They are, however, only a part of our nation's garden heritage.

We are fortunate to have many more magnificent gardens in America than can ever be illustrated in the pages of one book. Not included are such outstanding displays of plants and flowers as those at the University of Washington Arboretum in Seattle, Golden Gate Park in San Francisco, the Arnold Arboretum in Boston and the Tryon Palace Gardens in North Carolina, to name only a few worthy of a place in a collection of this kind.

Most of the gardens shown on these pages are the direct result of a compelling interest in plants by one dedicated individual. Here are the du Pont family's splendid creations at Longwood Gardens in Pennsylvania and at Winterthur in Delaware. Here is the hand-wrought beauty that Douglas Chandor created at White Shadows in Weatherford, Texas, as well as the special kind of executive skill and planning of Henry Shaw who was personally responsible for the establishment of the distinguished Missouri Botanical Gardens on his estate in St. Louis.

Opposite: One of the attractions at Duke Gardens in Somerville, New Jersey, is the Arizona Desert Garden featuring cacti and other succulents.

Below: In gardens such as the Governor's Palace Garden at Colonial Williamsburg, symmetry and constant geometric design are all important.

Gottscho-Schleisner, Inc.

Man has long derived pleasure and sustenance from the greenery of the gardens, jungles, grasslands, swamps and forests of the world.

In many cases great gardens have been founded upon an enthusiasm for one particular plant — an enthusiasm that grows to include related plants and, then, the subtleties of overall design. Bellingrath Gardens is the result of one man's interest in azaleas, Sherwood Gardens began with a display of tulips and, in the Hershey Rose Gardens and Arboretum, it was the love of roses that gave the garden its start. Sometimes the genesis of a great garden is the beauty of a particular site, a scenic vista, or a deep feeling for the land of one's ancestors.

An inspirational example of the latter is the devoted work and determination of Mr. and Mrs. J.J. Pringle Smith to bring Middleton Place, one of the treasures of the South, back to its original glory. Not only have they succeeded, they have made it a more beautiful estate than it had ever been before.

The need for continuity in the evolution of two gardens in this book was such that the owners, who had no heirs, passed their estates along with the requirement that the recipients change their names. Thomas Drayton II willed Magnolia-on-the-Ashley, near Charleston, South Carolina, to his grandson, John Grimke, on the condition that he take the name Drayton. John Grimke-Drayton complied, and Magnolia is now in its seventh generation in the same family, and still a classic Southern garden. Hampton National Historic Site in Towson, Maryland, is probably here for us to enjoy today because Charles Ridgely Carnan agreed to change his name to Charles Carnan Ridgely to meet the terms of his uncle's bequest. He inherited the estate, adopted the Ridgely coat of arms and made the gardens the loveliest of their time.

If we were dealing with architecture or philosophy, we could say that the gardens in this book were "humanist" in concept. They are the works of men — and women — inspired with a missionary zeal to find the best materials and, by their own lights, to create the most rewarding beauty with the means at hand. The means were often considerable and their efforts became significant and, in some cases, monumental.

These great estates evolved at a time when the tax structure allowed the tremendous expenditures required to create master-pieces of gardening and design. Sociologists might say that the estates were created at the expense of society. But they *were* created, and they exist today for the benefit of those who have the ability to see and appreciate. All of the gardens shown here are open to the public. Their beauty belongs to us all.

Can anyone who decries past extravagances seriously suggest that not to have created The Elms or Descanso Gardens or Dumbarton Oaks would have bettered the conditions of the day? The great gardens of the past were not causes, they were the effects of a particular time and place.

These gardens, expressions as they are of intense personal involvement and enthusiasm, show what can be done with single-minded interest and attention. It is not likely that, in this country, we can ever expect to do so much again — on such a vast scale. These are the last remnants of strong individual taste expanded to a maximum degree. Their history can be read in the text, and the

Above: The gardens at Dumbarton Oaks in Washington, D.C., are the result of meticulous planning by their designer, Beatrix Farrand, and former owners, Ambassador and Mrs. Robert Woods Bliss.

Left: In his essay, *Of Gardens,* Francis Bacon wrote: "Men come to build Stately sooner than to Garden Finely: as if Gardening were the Greater Perfection."

13

Reynolda Gardens in Winston-Salem, North
Carolina, has become in the last ten years,
a vital part of Wake Forest University.

pictures reveal the essence of their design. Their example can be an inspiration to us all.

The beauty of a garden is a balm to heart and mind. If, in looking upon these pages, you are impelled to visit but one great garden, your life will be enriched and your own garden the better for it. Ideas are contagious, and these gardens are great living catalogs of plants and plantings.

There are other fine estates that may not yet be opened to the public but few, if any, will be created in the future. We may get more parks — in fact we must. But if their size and design is largely controlled by committee, they will be as predictable and unexciting as all other products of group decision. The great things are done by inspired individuals.

The world-wide quest of a Mabel Choate, to find furnishings for her garden at Naumkeag, may never again be duplicated. And how, in the future, could we expect a committee to cater to the whimsy of a Bishop Chance and build wishing wells and stone gnomes and miniature stone lighthouses in a stream? We may very well say it is not for us, but we respect and revel in the fact that it *was* for him and he made it happen. The lesson is clear: Better to grow a dozen petunias with a passion than an acre of roses for the sake of convention.

To savor the unique quality of a great garden of magnificent scale is to realize that there is no adequate substitute for such an experience. Those who know what beautiful plantings among great spaces can do for the human senses, will not fail to support the preservation of other estates when such opportunities arise. The fine old places must not be lost forever. Gardening is a major art and worthy of our support.

One of the first to put the art of gardening in perspective was Francis Bacon. In his essay, *Of Gardens*, he wrote:

God Almighty first Planted a Garden. And indeed, it is the purest of Human pleasures. It is the Greatest refreshment to the Spirits of Man; without which Buildings and Pallaces are but Grosse Handy-Works: And a Man shall ever see, that when Ages grow to Civility and Elegance, Men come to build Stately sooner than to Garden Finely: As if Gardening were the Greater Perfection.

The validity of Bacon's thought is exemplified throughout this book. Many of the houses seem to be completely of another time. But the gardens are as fresh and lovely as tomorrow. They have a timeless quality that makes them, in Bacon's words, "the Greater Perfection."

Turn these pages slowly. Read the history of the gardens and study the pictures. This is the physical world at its best. And you can help to keep it so. Everyone who tends a plot of land is master of a garden. The design is in his hands and all of nature's forces at his call. An azalea knows not whether it is tended by Pierre du Pont or Joseph Smith. It responds only to proper care. Anyone can have a Winterthur in microcosm. To make your own estate a place of beauty, be it fifty front-feet or five acres, you have only to become as deeply interested and involved as those who made the gardens in this book.

But, in the end, we must understand that beauty is the least of it. Our very lives depend upon maintaining a workable balance of plants and people on this planet. Our fate is inexorably tied to the fate of the greenery in the gardens, jungles, grasslands, swamps and forests of the world. It is this, The Gardener's Point of View, that herein is encouraged and must finally prevail.

Biltmore House and Gardens in North Carolina are among the world's magnificent and lavish showplaces.

Azaleas, the outstanding flower at Bellingrath Gardens near Mobile, help to brighten the Great Lawn near the house.

Courtesy Bellingrath Gardens

CYPRESS GARDENS

Tradition and Beauty in the Carolina Low Country

Courtesy Charleston Trident Chamber of Commerce

Although much of the Gardens consists of
small connected lakes, there are many
woodland scenes of pines and white dogwoods.

Opposite: Built on an old plantation site
in 1927, Cypress Gardens has the beauty
characteristic of the Carolina Low Country.

Charleston, South Carolina, one of the most prosperous of the
early American port towns, sits on the fertile peninsula between
two broad rivers, the Ashley and the Cooper, which flow together to
form the Port of Charleston. From its very beginning, this has been
a focal point of American gardening. To the residents of Charleston
the garden has always been a place to live in, to be married in and
to enjoy the year around. Even now in the quiet early morning,
Charleston flower women still walk the narrow streets with rush
baskets full of swamp lilies. The Carolina springtime brings
thousands of visitors to see Charleston's trio of famous gardens:
Magnolia, Cypress and Middleton.

Naturalists and botanists have long admired the beauty of the
area. Early in the eighteenth century John and William Bartram,
the father and son famous for their work of collecting and
domesticating native American plants, made Charleston their
Southern headquarters. To William Bartram the Deep South was
"the very palace of Madame Flora." Later Banksia roses and
wisteria were brought here from China. The colorful poinsettia *(P.
pulcherrima)* was introduced by one of Charleston's most distinguished citizens, Joel Poinsett, U.S. Minister to Mexico. Dr.
Alexander Garden, the Scottish physician for whom the gardenia
(Gardenia jasminoides or cape jasmine) was named, made his home
in Charleston. And it was here that André Michaux, the famous
French botanist, brought the first camellias and azaleas to grow in
this hemisphere.

Along the two broad rivers flanking Charleston lie the Santee
swamplands, the Carolina Low Country where many of the greatest
antebellum plantations were built. Cedar Grove, Oak Forest, the
Elms, Tranquil Hill, Bloomfield and Crowfield — said to be the
most famous and beautiful of all — and the three Charleston
gardens: Cypress Gardens at Dean Hall, Magnolia-on-the-Ashley
and Middleton Place were built on the bounty of this rich land.

The cultivation of rice began here early in the seventeenth century
on the large acreage granted by the Crown. Hundreds of slaves were
brought in to cultivate this difficult but very profitable crop. The
planters, mostly British, used their wealth and large land holdings
to re-create, as nearly as possible, the style and pattern of English
manor life in this new land.

As one approaches the Santee swamplands outside of Charleston
there is a subtle change in the atmosphere. The low, flat marshland

Paul E. Cenereux

At Cypress the air is heavy with the
scent of azaleas, daphne, camellias and
wisteria along miles of breathtaking paths.

Opposite: In 1927, as two hundred men worked
cutting away the undergrowth, they
revealed a wealth of established cypresses.

gives an illusion of limitless space and distance. Low-hanging ropes
of Spanish moss filter the sunlight, blending substance and shadow.
There is a stillness in the air, heavy with heat and the scent of wildflowers. This is a land like no other. It has a character of its own
that penetrates the very bones of those who have become a part of
it. It is this compelling aspect of the Low Country that has kept
some people interested in maintaining and improving its unique
and haunting loveliness for as long as seven generations. Although
Cypress Gardens is relatively new it has the area's characteristic
beauty and is built on the site of an historic plantation. Respect for
tradition is an integral part of the appeal of this great garden.

Here are the dark, watery cypress forests which have woven
themselves into American history. Legend-deep, impenetrable
places, feared by the early settlers, they were the domain of the
Indian and only the bravest of the native trappers and woodsmen.
The trunks of the bald cypress *(Taxodium distichum)* rise straight
and tall from the water like the pillars of a giant cathedral, topped
with delicate green foliage. One of the earliest forms of vegetation
on this planet, they exude from their roots tannic acid which stains
the water around them a deep inky black. The roots also send up
"knees," solid protuberances that grow around the cypress' base
and add to its strange and striking appearance. Here in the
Southern coastal swamps this dramatic ancient tree has its last
foothold in the world. It was from the maze of such watery forests
that Francis Marion, the "Swamp Fox," would emerge to harry the
British during the Revolutionary War. The legends of fugitives and
hidden communities deep in these mysterious swamps are an
integral part of the folklore of the land.

Cypress Gardens, found twenty-four miles out of Charleston on
the Cooper River, was created on a typical cypress swamp. It covers
240 acres of lake and woodland. The tall, bald cypress, hung with
Spanish moss, and reflected in the dark waters gives the garden an
aura of mystery and beauty. But the greater beauty of Cypress
Gardens comes from the juxtaposition of the dark cypress to the
flaming colors of azalea and other flowers on the shore of the lake
and the islands. These somber waters, with their numerous deep
channels, have been likened to the canals of Venice.

The garden at Cypress is only forty years old; but the lake, a
major part of the garden, was the reservoir of Dean Hall, a rice
plantation where, before the Civil War, there were more than five
hundred slaves and workmen.

At Dean Hall, owned by Sir John Nesbitt of Dean, Scotland, the
rice crop flourished, and by 1842 it was described as a model
plantation. The large natural lake was channeled to irrigate the rice
fields and to serve as a reservoir. With the coming of the Civil War,
the slaves fled from Dean Hall, the buildings were destroyed and
the native growth began to take over.

It was not until 1927 that this land was reclaimed from the wild.
Benjamin R. Kittredge, then owner of Dean Hall, conceived the
idea of turning the 250 acres of lake and swampland into a garden. A
crew of some two hundred men worked for several years simply to

A. Devaney, Inc., N.Y. - Warren Brant

19

Courtesy Charleston Trident Chamber of Commerce

Photos: Paul E. Genereux

Above: Several years were needed simply to clear the tangled underbrush and debris from the lake and surrounding woodland.

Left: The somber waters of Cypress, with their numerous deep channels, have been likened to the canals of Venice.

Opposite: One of the first forms of vegetation known on earth, the bald cypress exudes tannic acid which stains the water a deep black.

21

Opposite: Footpaths encircle the dark watery cypress forests and cross over to give visitors a more intimate view of the flowers and trees.

In 1963 Cypress Gardens was given to the City of Charleston and is now operated by the City Council and a board of advisors.

Photos: Paul E. Genereux

clear the tangled underbrush and debris from the lake and surrounding woodland. Outside the area of the garden there is still the native swampland, giving today's visitor a sense of the tremendous undertaking it was to drain and improve this difficult terrain. Remember, too, that this was done before the advent of bulldozers, backhoes and other modern earthmoving equipment.

When the land was drained and filled, the workmen set out several thousand plants in the rich black soil — plants including the tender Indian azaleas that thrive in this mild climate; *Daphne odora*, the fragrant small bush from the Orient; narcissus in variety; sweet olive; and wisteria. The stars of the floral show are camellias, which open the blossoming season at Thanksgiving and carry it on as, one after the other, more than three hundred varieties come into spectacular bloom. The camellia was named by Linnaeus for Georg Josef Kamel, the Moravian Jesuit and horticulturist of the seventeenth century. Wherever it can be grown it has become a favorite. In the South it rivals the ever-present boxwood in popularity.

Nor were the native plants neglected. The two hundred gardeners cutting away the undergrowth revealed the wealth of established cypress trees and water gums. They left the supple-jack and cross-vine climbing their way into the tree tops, the tangles of golden Carolina jessamine, and one of the most beautiful Southern flowers, the little atamasco lily.

Today, when the gardens are in bloom, this is an earthly paradise of color and contrast; a fitting tribute to the work of Kittredge and his determined gardeners. One of the best ways to see Cypress is by water in the small craft paddled by stoic Low Country boatmen. The half-hour trip is of breathtaking beauty through miles of tall cypress and brilliant flowers, their impact enhanced immeasurably by reflection in the quiet black waters. The boat glides under arching white bridges, between the islands and the shore, that are twined with vines of the legend-haunted Cherokee rose. You hear the call of the yellow-throated warbler and see the staccato flight of a brilliant cardinal. For anyone interested in birds, Cypress Gardens is worth a visit on that score alone. On any fine spring day a sharp-eyed bird-watcher can count up to a hundred different species here. There are egrets, herons, hawks and the brilliant painted bunting, to name but a few. The air is heavy with the scent of azaleas, daphne, roses and wisteria. This is a unique and quiet place of impressive grandeur and beauty. Footpaths encircle the lake and cross over to the small islands to give the visitor a more intimate view of the plants, trees and flowers.

In 1963 Cypress Gardens was given to the City of Charleston and is now operated by the City Council and an independent board of advisors. And so it is that land once given by the Crown to a favored few — at the expense of many — now belongs to the Community for the pleasure and benefit of all.

Charleston, South Carolina

MIDDLETON PLACE GARDENS

Oldest Landscaped Garden in America

Middleton Place on the Ashley River stands in as sharp contrast to Cypress Gardens as midafternoon sunshine does to evening twilight. Here we find open well-tended formal gardens, including the terraced lawns, so unusual for the flat Carolina Low Country, sloping down past the twin lakes to the flat savannah and the wide sweep of the Ashley. This is the oldest landscaped garden in the United States, planted in the 1700's by Henry Middleton, President of the First Continental Congress. The garden wears its age like a regal mantle. This, perhaps, is inevitable for so much of its beauty derives from the continuity of its being in the same family for two centuries. In 1941 Middleton Place was awarded the Garden Club of America's coveted Bulkley Medal for "two hundred years of enduring beauty."

In Middleton's long and exciting history there is also the story of one of South Carolina's most notable families. The first record of the land was a warrant issued in 1675. In 1741 it came into the Middleton family. Henry Middleton was the owner of several large rice plantations, including The Oaks, Goose Creek, which he inherited from his forebears who were landholders here for many generations. The land that was to become Middleton Place was the dowry of Mary Williams who married Henry Middleton. Middleton began immediately to make the property into a place of beauty. He built the manor house, probably one of the most impressive of its day, on a site overlooking the Ashley River. Although the name of the man who designed this famous garden is not recorded, he certainly knew his profession and probably came from England. The park-like English style of landscape design was much favored in the colonies. English garden design at the time was greatly influenced by the great estates of France, and these in turn by the Italian villas. So what finally came to America was a happy amalgamation.

The original design for Middleton had many similarities to the gardens of Le Nôtre at Versailles. It took the labor of one hundred slaves working daily for about nine years to complete the formal garden stretching out to the north and east of the manor house to include a flower garden and a long narrow reflecting pool or canal. Here in the formal garden stood the giant oak tree, now called the Middleton Oak, which even before the colony's settlement had been used by the Indians as a trail marker and which now towers over the garden with a limb spread of some 145 feet. This noble tree is estimated to be nine hundred years old. It is not formally related to the design of the garden. It is simply there as a natural force. The

Courtesy Charleston Trident Chamber of Commerce

Middleton Gardens are the oldest landscaped gardens in America, dating from about 1741, but contain, in addition, many rustic areas.

Opposite: During the Revolutionary War, British soldiers looted Middleton Place and decapitated the garden's statues. Of the original statues, only a wood nymph by Johann Schadow remains.

carefully contrived plots and vistas go their own way, and the tree stands on its own.

The slope in front of the house is carved into a number of grassy terraces leading down to the two lakes, which were once part of the intricate system that irrigated nearby rice fields. These are the famous "butterfly lakes" ingeniously shaped to form the wings while the grassy lawn between the two lakes takes the shape of a butterfly's body.

When Middleton Place was first built, the primary means of transportation was not the roadway, which was impassable many months of the year, but the Ashley River. Each of the families along the river had its own boat furnished with cushions for comfort and canvas for shade. The slaves rowed them back and forth on their frequent visits between neighboring plantations. The visitor at Middleton would have approached the stately manor house by way of a path that began at the dock on the river beneath towering oak trees. It then led up between the two wings of the butterfly lakes through some 350 feet of spectacular beauty. Today the memorable experience of approaching the house from the river can be recaptured by walking through the great open parterre. Now beautifully lined with azaleas and other fine shrubs, in the eighteenth century it was planted primarily in green shrubbery and probably with topiary work.

When Henry Middleton resigned from the First Continental Congress, his son Arthur took over his post, becoming one of the first signers of the Declaration of Independence. Upon his father's death, Arthur Middleton assumed the upkeep of Middleton Place and did much to improve the already beautiful gardens. From Arthur the estate passed into the hands of his son Henry who was a Governor of South Carolina and later Minister to Russia. He was also a friend of the notable French botanist André Michaux. It was to Middleton Place that Michaux came when he visited South Carolina in the early 1780's, bringing with him the first camellias *(Camellia japonica)* ever to be planted in this country. Today this lovely flower grows abundantly at Middleton. Of the original four planted here by Michaux, there are three still standing, one with a trunk more than five feet in circumference and another more than twenty-five feet tall.

From Henry Middleton the estate passed on to his son Williams who devoted himself to the expansion of the gardens including the planting of many choice azaleas. It was he who started the first so-called Indian azalea *(Azalea indica)* here. This native of China and Formosa is more properly named *Rhododendron simsi.* (All azaleas, of course, are of the genus *Rhododendron.*)

However, the magnificence of the original gardens has not remained unimpaired throughout its long life. By the end of the

Paul E. Genereux

The park-like English style of landscape and garden design, influenced by the great French estates, was much favored in the colonies.

Opposite: The Rice Mill Pond at Middleton has been recently renewed and is now one of the most beautiful spots in the Gardens.

The slope in front of the house is carved into a number of grassy terraces leading down to the famous butterfly lakes.

Below: After inheriting the estate in 1924, J.J. Pringle Smith, his wife and several gardeners worked and reworked the grounds until the grass regained its lush green.

Photos: Gottscho-Schleisner, Inc.

Paul E. Genereux

Above: Henry Middleton conducted America's first Sunday School for slaves on the upper floor of the Old Spring House.

Right: The dark water of the Rice Mill Pond reflects the beauty of ancient oaks along its banks.

Courtesy Charleston Trident Chamber of Commerce

Gottscho-Schleisner, Inc.

Above: The Old Rice Mill, built in 1741 and now a museum, was originally powered by tidewater allowed to back up off the Ashley.

Below: This rustic portion of the garden was planted with 35,000 azaleas which add their bright colors to wisteria and pine trees.

Courtesy Charleston Trident Chamber of Commerce

nineteenth century what was left of Middleton's beauty and impressive formality was overgrown and deserted. Had it not been for the efforts of J.J. Pringle Smith, a direct descendant of Henry Middleton, who inherited the estate in 1924, and his wife Heningham, the serene beauty that was once Middleton's might have been lost forever.

When Mr. and Mrs. Smith first went to see their inheritance, they found only the remains of the great estate. An extraordinary number of misfortunes had befallen Middleton Place before the end of the nineteenth century. The original house was a three-story brick manor in the Georgian style. In 1755, as the story goes, Arthur Middleton was warned one day by a messenger that his house was on fire. After composing himself, he wet a finger and held it up to the wind. Finding that the wind was blowing unfavorably, he suggested that the house be allowed to burn. Mrs. Middleton, however, took charge and the fire was extinguished. Two new wings were added to the house at that time.

Because Henry Middleton and his son Arthur were so strongly against the British in the Revolutionary War, Middleton became a sure target for British soldiers who looted the house, leaving chaos behind. They even decapitated the statues in the garden. Of the original statues only one remains, a wood nymph by Johann Gottfried Schadow which rested in the Gibbes Art Gallery in Charleston during the Civil War, but which has now been returned to its original site in the garden.

In 1865, during the Civil War, Middleton Place again became the target for an advancing army. The slaves fled and the rice crop was left to ruin. In 1886 Middleton Place was shaken by an earthquake and by the turn of the century all that remained was an overgrown tangle of weeds choking out the flowers and plant life. When Mr. and Mrs. J.J. Pringle Smith took over the estate in 1927, Mrs. Smith was an "outsider," a Virginia girl who knew little about flowers and gardening. But she determined to become a garden expert. With the help of several gardeners, the couple set out to restore the estate to its original beauty. The south wing of the manor house was prepared for residence. The grounds were worked and reworked until the grass regained its original lushness. The ponds were rebuilt and refilled, the hedges clipped and pruned.

In addition to restoring the garden, the Smiths have made several striking improvements. There is now a rare Camellia Garden and a dazzling hillside planting of 35,000 azaleas. Recently a Cypress pond has been developed and, beside the dock on the Ashley River, the old rice mill pond and what used to be the rice mill have been renewed. The lower floor of the mill, now completely restored, has been made into a museum. Middleton Place is a garden that has developed beautifully under the enlightened attention of many generations of a family devoted to the finest traditions of the South.

Opposite: In 1941 the Garden Club of America awarded Middleton the coveted Bulkley Medal for "two hundred years of enduring beauty."

MAGNOLIA GARDENS

"None So Beautiful as This"

Gottscho-Schleisner, Inc.

Magnolia Gardens, with its twenty-five acres of flower gardens, three lakes and sixteen acres of oak-planted lawns, is prized by connoisseurs.

Opposite: British author John Galsworthy once said of Magnolia Gardens, "It is a kind of paradise which has wandered down, a miraculously enchanted wilderness."

Magnolia-on-the-Ashley is the most famous of the Charleston trio of gardens, and it is also considered by many to be the loveliest. Magnolia combines the strange, unearthly beauty, the dark cypress-filled waters and stunning color contrasts of Cypress Gardens with the open green lawns and towering oaks of Middleton Place. It takes its name from the row of evergreen magnolia trees *(Magnolia grandiflora)* that once lined the walk from the Ashley River to the manor house. The last of these magnificent trees along the avenue died in 1957, but fortunately many other large magnolias with broad wax-polished leaves and fragrant cuplike blossoms survive throughout the gardens. The fame of Magnolia-on-the-Ashley, however, is based on the beauty and great variety of azaleas and other flowers planted by the Reverend John Grimke-Drayton in the mid-nineteenth century.

Though it has only been planted in its present style since shortly before the Civil War, Magnolia — with its twenty-five acres of flower gardens, three beautiful lakes, and sixteen acres of oak-planted lawns — has received the accolades of many established garden connoisseurs down through the years.

John Galsworthy, the famous British novelist and playwright, considered himself something of an expert of the subject of gardens. He had, indeed, visited many world-famous gardens: La Mortala in Italy, the Generaliffe in Granada, Boboli in Florence, Conception in Málaga, and nearer home, Versailles in France and England's Hampton Court. Yet of Magnolia he declared, "none in the world is so beautiful as this." He called Magnolia "a kind of paradise which has wandered down, a miraculously enchanted wilderness."

In the Baedeker guide for 1900 there are only three places in America considered worthy of three stars — the Grand Canyon, Niagara Falls and Magnolia Gardens.

The Magnolia Plantation, like the other two Charleston plantations with outstanding gardens, has a long and fascinating history. In 1676 the land was first mentioned in the South Carolina land records as "a parcel of land butting on the Ashley River and a cane and bryer patch." The land was granted to one Morris Matthews.

We seem to have no record of the second owner. However, the third was Thomas Drayton, a planter of English descent, who emigrated in 1671 from Barbados and began life in the new land.

Gottscho-Schleisner, Inc.

In the Baedeker guide for 1900 only three places in America are given three stars: the Grand Canyon, Niagara Falls and Magnolia.

Opposite: The dark waters of the swamp reflect like plate-glass mirrors, echoing bridges, trees and flowers.

The original Magnolia house he built was considered to be one of the most stately in all of Carolina. Destroyed by fire shortly after the Revolution, this house was replaced by one of cypress which also burned during the Civil War.

John Davis, a young Englishman who tutored Thomas Drayton's children, described the Carolina spring in the records he kept while he was teaching here in the Low Country: "The borders of the forest were covered with the blossoms of the dog-wood, of which the white flowers caught the eye from every part; and often was to be seen with the red-bud tree, which purpled the adjacent woods with its luxuriant branches; while not infrequently shrubs of jessamine, intermixed with wood-bine, lined the road for several miles." And he goes on to comment on the bird life, which is still an important aspect of the special quality of the Southern spring. "The feathered choir began to warble their strains, and from every tree was heard the song of the red-bird, of which the pauses were filled by the mocking-bird, who either imitated the note with exquisite precision, or poured forth a ravishing melody of its own."

Of Magnolia-on-the-Ashley specifically he says only: "The garden of Mr. Drayton's mansion led to the banks of the Ashley River which after a rapid course of twenty miles discharged itself into the Atlantic."

That Magnolia had beautiful formal gardens at that time, however, is almost a certainty. Flowerdale, a small formal garden which is still to be seen here was laid out long before the Civil War. There are some fine old specimen plants in this garden, including a collection of magnificent Chinese yews and a giant camellia, thirty feet high.

The present design of Magnolia Gardens was begun before the Civil War by the Reverend John Grimke-Drayton. His grandfather, Thomas Drayton II, willed the plantation to him on the condition that he take the name Drayton. Not long after the newly named Grimke-Drayton became master of Magnolia, he became ill and was advised by his physician, to "take to the soil to dig."

His first project as a gardener was a modest one. He planted two rose bushes, one red and one white, on either side of the ivy-covered steps that formed the entrance to the earlier Magnolia manor. From this he steadily progressed to more ambitious plantings.

Around 1840, several rhododendron *(R. indicum)* were imported for planting in the Philadelphia area. The chill Philadelphia winter proved to be too much for this delicate species and Grimke-Drayton was prevailed upon to see how it would grow at Magnolia. This proved to be the perfect climate and the beautiful rhododendron have been a special feature of Magnolia Gardens ever since.

In 1848 the Reverend Mr. Grimke-Drayton planted the first Indian azaleas, then called *Azalea indica,* to grow in America. These lovely flowering plants were brought here by the French botanist, André Michaux and have since been more accurately identified as *Rhododendron indicum,* and as *Rhododendron simsi.* The Indian

Winston Pote from A. Devaney, N.Y.

Grimke-Drayton blended unique native growth of the Southern United States, such as Spanish moss *(above),* with azaleas and camellias *(below),* native to China and Japan.

Opposite: The dramatic quality of the gardens derives from the ingenious juxtaposing of flower colors to the grays of the swamp.

Paul E. Genereux

Gottscho-Schleisner, Inc.

Above: Bald cypress roots send up solid protuberances called "knees." The tree has its last foothold in the Southern coastal swamps.

Below: Wisteria, banksia roses and giant oaks combine to make Magnolia Gardens a floral wonderland famous in America and Europe.

Courtesy Charleston Trident Chamber of Commerce

azalea has flowers, usually single, up to three inches across in clear tones of pink or red. Many fine hybrids have been developed from this species combined with others. He also planted great stands of the *Camellia japonica*, which was already beautifying the neighboring plantation of Middleton, and bringing to Magnolia-on-the-Ashley a brilliance previously unknown.

Azaleas and camellias were not a part of the garden's original color scheme. Only Fraser's lilies (swamp lilies, white and frail along the edge of the water), Carolina jessamine and the great Southern magnolia were native here.

As Grimke-Drayton's garden grew he displayed an ingenious dramatic flair for juxtaposing brilliant flower colors to the dark grays and greens of the swamp. In Kew Gardens, though azaleas grow in abundance, a sign near the azalea plantations reads, "azaleas in their highest glory are to be found in Magnolia Gardens, near Charleston, South Carolina, U.S.A." The azaleas are magnificent, to be sure. But azaleas and rhododendron grow beautifully in many other parts of the world. The incomparable impact that they have at Magnolia-on-the-Ashley is because of the dramatic setting of swamp cypress rising from the dark waters that reflect the brilliant flower colors as though in a plate-glass mirror. Shortly after the Civil War, Grimke-Drayton opened the gardens to the public.

Today the visitor at Magnolia still finds the long row of towering live oaks bordering the road to Magnolia Manor. There are broad green lawns and near the River Walk a maze of paths cross and criss-cross where blazing reds and pinks arrest the eye at every point. The dark waters of the cypress swamp reflect the color, echoing the already dramatic image of white azalea, green cypress and rustic bridges. The general shape of this garden is fan-like with azalea-lined walks radiating outward from the house.

After the first dazzling effect of the azalea plants wears off, one begins to notice others that give Magnolia such satisfying depth and completeness. The list of trees and shrubs planted here is a long one: sweet bay, arborvitae, dwarf boxwood, dogwood, cedar, euonymus, holly, California redwood, willow, sycamore and beech.

And there are flowers, which may be effaced at first by the beauty of the azaleas, but which have a distinctive charm of their own. Sylphide and Cherokee roses twine with wisteria high in the branches of the trees. Sweet olive, jessamine, myrtle and many favorite garden flowers add to the garden's enchanting beauty. Again it is the combination of these flowers with the natural setting of cypress swamp, which can in no way be duplicated by man-made design, that gives the garden its extraordinary appeal. It was Grimke-Drayton's genius to blend azaleas and camellias native to China and Japan with unique native growth of South Carolina to create a whole much greater than the sum of the parts.

And in a grove of tall oaks there is a marble tomb. Carved into the stone are these words: "Reverend John Grimke-Drayton 1815-91. Creator of this garden, the spirit of which speaks more eloquently than words of the vision which was his."

Opposite: Near the River Walk, a maze of paths cross and criss-cross where blazing purples and reds arrest the eye at every point.

Williamsburg, Virginia

COLONIAL WILLIAMSBURG GARDENS

Beauty in the Present and Insight into the Past

Time, in Colonial Williamsburg, stands still, locked serenely in a living restoration of the town as it was in the eighteenth century. Along the broad, shaded streets, the horse-drawn carriages and costumed tradesmen return us to the days when Virginia was still an English colony, that exciting era when such patriots as Patrick Henry, George Washington and Thomas Jefferson raised their voices against bondage to the mother country.

The gardens of this early American town, as well as its houses and shops, exemplify Williamsburg's motto, "That the future may learn from the past." And learn we can from the varied uses of plant material and superb architectural proportions of the gardens. For the backyard gardener, faced with the problem of enhancing his limited space there is much to be learned from the residential gardens of Williamsburg, similar in their formality, but each distinctive in planting and design. There is no question that these early American settlers had something invaluable to teach us all about the gentle art of gardening.

While the Puritans of New England still struggled with their stony farms and rigorous climate, the Virginia colonists were beginning to grow the valuable crop of tobacco in the warm sunlight of a fertile land. By the end of the seventeenth century, there were prosperous plantations the length and breadth of the Tidewater area. The first colonists established their capital at Jamestown, beside the river where they landed. Later it was moved inland to the more healthful climate of Middle Plantation, renamed Williamsburg in honor of King William III, located on the highest ridge between the James and York Rivers.

Williamsburg in 1699 was a quiet town, home of the colony's first university, The College of William and Mary, where Thomas Jefferson, John Marshall, Benjamin Harrison, Edmund Randolph, John Tyler and others from as far away as Maryland and New York explored the world of ideas and graduated to important posts in a growing country. Sir Francis Nicholson directed the building of the town, where each citizen was allowed one-half acre of land. Each house was required by law to be exactly six feet from the street and surrounded by a fence four and one-half feet high to keep out strayed cattle and horses.

Throughout most of the year, even after becoming the capital, Williamsburg showed the quiet facade of an English country town and the population never exceeded 1,800 in all. Twice each year, however, during "publick times," the town overflowed with people.

A gnarled paper mulberry stands near the Carter-Saunders House, attesting to the antiquity of the reconstructed town.

Opposite: On Duke of Gloucester Street in re-created Colonial Williamsburg, the Bryan Garden displays topiary accents.

In the Orlando Jones Garden, an enclosing tree box hedge provides a background for gaily colored tulips.

Opposite: Glinting in the sunlight over the garden exit of the Governor's Palace is the regal, stately coat of arms of the House of Hanover and King George II.

Manicured topiary and evergreen parterres add their color to that of tulips and asters in the Governor's Palace Garden.

The court convened, the legislature met and there was tobacco to be bought and sold. Planters and burgesses brought their ladies for a taste of city culture, and people from every line of trade converged on the capital. Merchants trotted out their finest wares, the best to be had in the latest style direct from England. Street fairs were held with races and games. Anyone with anything to trade or sell found his way to Williamsburg for this exciting event.

During such times the Governor's Palace opened its tall wrought-iron gates to admit the crowds of gaily dressed men and women in liveried coaches for dances and other festivities. Thus it became a favored gathering place and was later to be known as "the second capitol of the colony," because of the political activity that went on there. Raleigh Tavern was thrown open at the governor's command for people of "quality."

As the town prospered, houses and shops sprang up. The first theatre in America was built on the east side of the Palace Green. George Washington, while still a young planter, loved the theatre and wrote in his diary after one visit, "Reach'd Williamsburg before Dinner, and went to the Play in the Afternoon." The town's Bruton Parish Church became the religious center for the colony.

For eighty-one years this thriving capital served as the center of culture and political life in the colony. It was a time of increasing independence as the colonists, from New York to Charleston, chafed under England's strictures. In 1780, during the Revolutionary War, the capital was moved to Richmond, more centrally located and safer from possible future attack. The Governor's Palace burned to the ground shortly thereafter, and new buildings were later constructed on the site. The face of Williamsburg changed as the old buildings deteriorated, burned and were torn down and new ones constructed.

Had it not been for the dream of one man, Dr. W.A.R. Goodwin, Rector of Bruton Parish Church, the Williamsburg of colonial times might have disappeared completely under the relentless tides of change. In 1926 Dr. Goodwin met with John D. Rockefeller, Jr., who agreed to finance what was to become the initial phase of the restoration of the old capital. After meticulous research, eighty-five of the buildings which had survived from the eighteenth century were carefully preserved and restored. Along broad Duke of Gloucester Street and within the bounds of the 173-acre Historic Area, the old buildings and properties were beautifully restored. These properties reflect the lives and times of colonial Virginians, from the wealthy plantation owner with a town house to the tradesmen, craftsmen, indentured servants and slaves, who formed the bulk of the population in eighteenth-century Williamsburg. A permanent endowment was set up by Mr. Rockefeller before his death in 1960, to guarantee the continuance of this worthy work.

In re-creating Williamsburg's gardens, as in restoring its buildings, every precaution was taken to be as authentic as possible. No flower or shrub has been planted here that did not grow in this country before 1800. This task was made more difficult by the fact that though many of the same plants grow in this country now as then, they have been improved and hybridized far beyond anything the settlers knew. The original plants were in some cases nearly extinct. Over ninety residential gardens are now completed in Williamsburg. Of these, twenty-five are open daily, and the rest by appointment

The tulip was the most popular garden flower in colonial
Williamsburg and shared space with clove pinks and larkspur.

The Governor's Palace, where boxwood is the shrub most often
used for topiary, as seen from the northwest.

The Bryan Garden features dwarf and tree boxwood and includes a special topiary accent in the form of a setting hen.

The tightly designed garden at the Powell-Waller House uses box and holly extensively. Tulips and flowering dogwood add their color.

for special tours. Gardens were an integral part of colonial living — both flower gardens for the beauty they afforded against the harshness of the surrounding wilderness, and vegetable and herb gardens for the food they provided. Literature on the subject was scarce. A book by Philip Miller, *The Gardener's Dictionary*, was a popular import from England. It was rivaled in favor around 1775 by John Randolph's *Treatise on Gardening*, which was more suitable for Virginia's gardeners.

There are three types of gardens found in Williamsburg. Most common is the small formal garden adjoining the frame or brick houses on the half-acre lots ordained by colonial law. It is easy enough to see why the citizens of colonial Williamsburg preferred their formal gardens, a style brought to its peak in England by King William and Queen Mary, to the more informal gardens that were favored in England by the end of the eighteenth century. There was "nature" enough surrounding the colonists to make them welcome the confines of their own small gardens filled with flowers and planted in a way that reminded them of home.

The gardens formed part of the architecture of each lot. Behind the house, for the sake of ventilation, the outbuildings, called "dependencies," such as a kitchen, laundry, wellhead, dairy, workshop, smokehouse and "necessaries" or privies, ranged neatly around a service yard of brick or marl. The centrally located garden was a bright spot of color. Green hedges bordered beds of tulips, foxgloves, phlox or other favorite flowers.

A hedging that was slow-growing, easy to care for, and able to withstand the hot sun as well as the Virginia frosts in winter was a necessity. The plant best suited was English boxwood of both the dwarf and tree varieties. Also used were bayberry, American yaupon and other holly varieties. The art of topiary, popular in the colony, most often took the shape of decorative balls and squares; though in some places the more ambitious animal shapes were used, such as the large replica of a setting hen in the Bryan Garden across from Bruton Parish Church. During the winter the basic form of the gardens was maintained by the geometry of the hedges. In summer the tangy scent of the boxwood foliage was in the air and the flower beds were bright with color.

The tulip was the most popular garden flower in colonial Williamsburg, as it was at the time in England. Dozens of multicolored Dutch Kaiserkrooms and other varieties joined the old traditional English roses, clove pinks, larkspur and hollyhocks. Though Virginia gardens were English in design, they soon took on a character that was essentially American. Native dogwood, redbud, black-eyed Susan, phlox, coreopsis, gallardia were planted beside the English imports. The shade trees, more necessary here than they were in the cooler British climate, were American. Elm, sycamore, hemlock, red cedar *(Juniperus virginiana)*, the scarlet oak *(Quercus coccinea)* and the ever popular Southern magnolia *(M. grandiflora)* were planted close around the houses for the comfort of their cooling shade. There are so many kinds of trees and shrubs that one can think of Williamsburg as an arboretum in which there happens to be a colonial village.

For the garden-conscious colonist there soon became available a wealth of foreign imports. The paper mulberry that develops such a picturesque trunk as it matures came from the Orient about 1750. The horse-chestnut was introduced from Europe in 1736, and the

Photos: Courtesy Colonial Williamsburg

Much of historic Williamsburg's appeal derives from the meticulous authenticity of its re-created gardens and reconstructed houses.

The gardens at Colonial Williamsburg, such as this one at the Deane House, rely heavily on the sharp geometric patterns of evergreens.

The greatest source of variety at Williamsburg is the way evergreens are used and combined with other plants.

The formal boxwood garden at the Wythe House has a central walk which was uncovered during archeological excavations.

Gottscho-Schleisner, Inc.

Courtesy Colonial Williamsburg

crape myrtle, now so much a part of Southern gardens, came from China in 1747. Even the ever present boxwood was introduced from the Mediterranean during early colonial times. These and others were brought to Virginia to become as much a part of the local scene as the fields of cotton and tobacco.

Beyond the formal gardens were the stables and coach house with their adjoining paddock and maintenance buildings. Here, too, were the vegetable gardens and the fruit trees. Though the settlers found the native strawberries, blueberries and wild grapes excellent and in profusion, the American fruit trees such as crab apple and pawpaw compared unfavorably to the European. Fruit trees were important as a source of cider and other drinks, so the apples, pears, plums, quince, cherry, peaches, apricots and persimmons were imported. Dwarf and espaliered fruit trees were also used for their decorative value in areas of limited space.

Another kind of garden design in Williamsburg is exemplified by the unmatched splendor of the grounds around the Governor's Palace. This is one of the few remaining perfect examples of the eighteenth-century garden. Begun under the supervision of Governor Alexander Spotswood in 1713, it was an extravagant attempt (as was the governor's mansion itself) to match the grandeur of the great European estates. This was largely accomplished, though disgruntled Williamsburg citizens, taxed several times for its construction, finally dubbed the governor's residence "the Palace."

The Governor's Palace, guarded by the royal Lion and Unicorn of England, faces the Palace Green, a carpet of lush grass as far as one can see. Thomas Jefferson once remarked in his writing that the catalpa trees lining the Palace Green were spaced exactly one hundred feet apart. These lovely trees (Catalpa bignonioides) have been replanted in just this fashion.

Behind the Palace, the doors of the large supper room open onto a long, formal garden elegantly laid out with sixteen boxwood diamonds accented with cones of clipped boxwood at each corner. Twelve large cylindrical yaupon hollies stretch toward the lower part of the garden. A carpet of periwinkle (Vinca minor) forms a textured backdrop for spring scilla, daffodils, crocus and hyacinth. Though garden ornaments were uncommon in the colonies, this garden contains lead finials and urns, and wooden Chippendale-style benches. On a lower level are boxwood topiary, pleached beech arbors, and long flower beds planted with tulips in the Dutch manner. The entire garden is surrounded by brick walls, fences and hedging.

North from this garden lie the fields which once sheltered the governor's deer — herds that roamed wild on the wooded acres. To the right is the plain parterre, a greensward which could be used for lawn bowls. And to the left lie a series of other compartmented gardens for fruit, herbs and vegetables. There is a boxwood parterre; a holly maze, unrivaled by any except that of Hampton Court after which it is patterned; a mount, customary in large eighteenth-century gardens, (concealing an ice house); and the "falling gardens" sloping gently down to a canal. Governor Spotswood must have been criticized for the expense of these gardens, for in 1718 he is recorded as telling the General Assembly that "if the Assembly did not care to be at the Expence of the Fish Pond and Falling Gardens," he would pay for them himself.

Courtesy Colonial Williamsburg

The third type of Williamsburg garden is that of the George Wythe house. The owner is probably better remembered as Thomas Jefferson's law teacher than as a signer of the Declaration of Independence, and it was at his gracious board that the young Tom Jefferson dined and listened and learned his lessons in the law. The Wythe house and garden, built along the lines of a Southern plantation, occupied two city lots facing on the Palace Green near Bruton Church. The main formal garden, constructed on the axis of the central hallway in the house, is a bowling green thickly carpeted with grass and surrounded with boxwood hedges and topiary accents. Fruit and kitchen gardens along one side of this central mall balance neatly with outbuildings along the other. An herb garden south of the main house has boxwood hedges and topiary work at each corner. At the west end, a pleached arbor of American hornbeam *(Carpinus caroliniana)* completes the design.

Of the important Williamsburg gardens, though unfortunately it no longer exists for viewing, probably the most memorable is the garden of Colonel John Custis whose daughter-in-law, Martha Dandridge Custis, later married George Washington. Custis moved to Williamsburg from Arlington on the Eastern Shore to be near the capitol and his duty as a Councilor of the Colony. For twenty years he worked to build a garden that was one of the loveliest in the colony. His interest in the subject led him to import specimens of the finest plants from England and Europe. Through his friend, Peter Collinson, a London wool draper and amateur botanist, he met the famous plantsman, John Bartram, of Philadelphia, and the three kept up a long correspondence which has since proved a valuable record of gardening and horticulture in colonial times.

A trip to Williamsburg offers more than its splendid beauty for the eye. It reveals an insight into the character of a period when the basic tenets of our democracy were being formed. Here the beauty of plants and unity of design was an integral part of the colonial capital. And who is to say that this satisfying and stable environment did not have its effect on the momentous events that were soon to follow.

Prized for its dwarf box collection, the Ludwell-Paradise House garden stresses holly, spring bulbs and summer flowering shrubs. The house was built around 1700.

Charlottesville, Virginia

MONTICELLO GARDENS

The Living Heritage of Early Virginia

There is little doubt that in the annals of American horticulture, Thomas Jefferson ranks among such great plantsmen as John Bartram, Jr., of Pennsylvania and William Drayton of South Carolina, both of whom were his friends and correspondents. Although most famous as author of the Declaration of Independence and third President of the United States, Jefferson was a man of many parts. Architect, educator, scientist, philosopher, he considered himself foremost an agrarian. In 1811 he wrote to his friend, the artist Charles Willson Peale, "No occupation is so delightful to me as the culture of the earth, and no culture comparable to that of the garden . . . . But though an old man, I am but a young gardener."

Jefferson made many contributions to agriculture in the United States. He introduced the concept of contour plowing and encouraged the use of the new plants he obtained during his travels abroad, as well as plants collected on the Lewis and Clark expedition to the West which he initiated. So important did he consider his introduction of dry rice and olive trees to South Carolina that he wrote at that time, "The greatest service which can be rendered any country is to add an useful plant to its culture." There are many today, however, who consider Jefferson's masterful landscape plans for his home, and for the University of Virginia at nearby Charlottesville, were as great a service, particularly in their influence on other designers.

After Jefferson's death, his Virginia home, Monticello, was sold in order to meet family debts, and before long the gardens became overgrown and disappeared. The estate was later purchased, however, by the Thomas Jefferson Memorial Foundation. During 1939-1940, the Garden Club of Virginia, using funds earned from its annual Historic Garden Week, restored the Monticello gardens. The work was meticulously done through research of Jefferson's own garden notes and correspondence and the books he was known to have read on the subject.

Even with the authenticity of the restoration, Monticello appears very much a part of the present. Jefferson had ideas remarkably advanced for his time and he continued to improve upon his designs throughout his lifetime. Jefferson loved Virginia and for all of his long life drew strength from the hills and woods of Monticello. As a young man he envisioned building a home atop a small, wooded mountain that was part of his father's Albemarle holdings. To the north the mountain commanded a view of the majestic Blue Ridge Mountains, and its southern exposure faced the wooded valley of

The Garden Club of Virginia meticulously restored the Monticello gardens during 1939 and 1940, using Jefferson's own garden notes.

Opposite: When Thomas Jefferson inherited his father's Albemarle holdings in 1757, he set about at once to build his now famous and admired mansion, Monticello.

In 1806, Jefferson wrote to his friend William Hamilton that he planned for "trees of the loftiest statures" to provide needed shade.

Albemarle. In 1757 he inherited the thousand-acre property, and as soon as the top of the hill was leveled and a road built up to it, he began building his famous mansion.

When Jefferson began Monticello in 1769, he was an accomplished gardener and was well read on all points of agriculture. By 1765, when he was twenty-two, he had already been favorably impressed by the new British style of naturalistic gardens through reading such volumes as William Shenstone's *Collected Works* and Thomas Whately's *Observations on Modern Gardening.* In 1766, while living where he was born, at Shadwell, another of his father's estates, he started to compile his own *Garden Book.* Throughout his busy years as statesman and administrator he recorded here his observations of nature and notes on improving Monticello and his other holdings.

Very little is known of the first years of gardening at Monticello. There is no indication that the flower borders which Jefferson sketched for his *Garden Book* around 1772 were ever actually planted. We can only assume that the responsibilities of running the house and the farm kept Jefferson and his staff too busy for the art of gardening. Undoubtedly there were flowers at Monticello during these years, for Jefferson records in his notes for 1782 (a slow year), the budding of hyacinths, narcissus, jonquils, anemones, iris, nasturtiums, tulips, peonies, lilies, sweet Williams, hollyhocks and roses. The planting must have been informal, if not haphazard, because no plans for flower gardens are recorded until 1793.

During Jefferson's long absence, between 1782 and 1792, nothing of note was accomplished at Monticello. As Ambassador to France (1784-1789), however, he was able to visit the gardens of Europe and his tour of English gardens with his friend John Adams, then Ambassador to England, convinced him that, "The gardening in that country is the article in which it surpasses all the earth." He was continually sending new specimens home for American plantsmen to try, and he often requested plants from America, especially his favorite "paccans" for his friends in Europe.

It was not until late in Jefferson's second term as President that the gardens of his Virginia home, as we know them today, were laid out. By this time the trees planted when the mansion was built had reached maturity. Jefferson wrote in 1806 to his friend William Hamilton of Philadelphia praising the British naturalistic gardens and stating his intention to use this style at Monticello. He spoke also of the need for shade in a Virginia garden and told his friend that he planned for "trees of the loftiest statures" (already planted here), trimmed high as their forms would bear so as to make the necessary shade and also to give the appearance of an open park. These trees should be thickly underplanted, he said, with shrubs, "especially evergreens," red cedar made to grow in a bush, evergreen privet, pyrocanthus, kalmia and Scotch broom.

In June 1807, Jefferson wrote to his eldest granddaughter, Anne Cary Randolph, describing the oval flower beds he planned for the West Lawn. These four oval beds, restorations of which can be seen today at Monticello, were to be planted with pinks *(Dianthus chinensis),* sweet Williams, double poppies, scarlet lychnis *(Lychnis*

Above: Jefferson considered himself an agrarian above all: "No occupation is so delightful to me as the culture of the earth...."

Below: The family name of the flowering dogwood derives from a bark extract used in England at one time to wash dogs with mange.

Trees — mountain ash, paper mulberry, tulip and Lombardy poplars, purple beech, lilac — are as important to garden design as flowers.

chalcedonica), cardinal flowers *(Lobelia cardinalis)*, the flowering pea of Arkansas (from Captain Lewis), tulips, double anemones, *Sprekelia formosissima* or St. James lily, and ranunculus, as well as specimens of *Jeffersonia binata,* named for Jefferson by Philadelphia botanist, Benjamin Smith Barton. Many of these bloom in shades of red, and it is likely that Jefferson planned for masses of red flowers. The "round-about" or walkway which circles the West Lawn, was also designed at this time, but was not completed until later.

During this period while he was in Washington Jefferson missed his growing family and the simple, pastoral life of Monticello. Often when a wagon load of goods from the estate was delivered he would send it back loaded with cuttings from a nearby Georgetown nursery. Jefferson's letters to his grandchildren at the time are filled with notes on the birds and flowers he observed in Washington and with questions about the growing things they saw in Virginia.

Anne Randolph was a knowledgeable gardener and Jefferson gave her the responsibility of looking after the gardens at Monticello. Another granddaughter, Ellen Randolph Coolidge, wrote in later years:

I remember well when he (Jefferson) first returned to Monticello, how immediately he began to prepare new beds for his flowers. He had these beds laid off on the lawn, under the windows, and many a time I have run after him when he went out to direct the work, accompanied by one of his gardeners, generally Wormley, armed with a spade and hoe, while he himself carried the measuring line. I was too young to aid him, except in a small way, but my sister, Mrs. Bankhead (Anne Randolph) . . . was his active and useful assistant . . . . Then when the flowers were in bloom, and we were in ecstasies over the rich purple and crimson, or pure white, or delicate lilac, or pale yellow of the blossoms, how he would sympathize in our admiration, or discuss with my mother and elder sister new groupings and combinations and contrasts.

Within the serpentine walk or round-about circling the West Lawn, a continuous border of mixed flowers was planted. In the restored beds, however, the border was divided into narrow beds, ten feet in length, each containing a separate planting of bellflowers, African marigolds *(Tagetes erecta)*, white poppies and other favorites of the day. Between these beds, which were curved around the carpet of carefully kept lawns, were planted redbud, mountain ash, paper mulberry, tulip and Lombardy poplars, purple beech, lilac, mock orange and other trees and shrubs that are as important to the design as the flowers themselves.

Though many years have passed since Monticello was the scene of such happy activity, the Virginia Garden Club's diligent research and careful restoration, has returned to us a Monticello that vividly recalls the famous man and his garden-loving family. As Jefferson did each year, we can anticipate the first blooming of the sweet Williams, the gay hyacinths of many hues, the bright scarlet cardinal flowers, poppies, pinks, tuberoses and the rainbow of flower color that takes us through the season. We can, as did the guests in Jefferson's day, promenade the round-about, enjoying the bright beds of flowers, the magnificent house and the views beyond — north to the haze of the Blue Ridge and south to the valley of the Albemarle. We come easily to understand why Jefferson loved this mountain home more than any other place on earth.

In the United States, tree magnolias sometimes reach heights of ninety feet, spreading their fragrant blooms over wide areas.

The restored beds within the round-about circling the West Lawn are planted in ten — foot lengths, each with its own flower.

Durham, North Carolina

SARAH P. DUKE MEMORIAL GARDENS

A Secluded Valley Adjoining a Campus

Botanical gardens have become an important aspect of some American university campuses where they form an integral part of campus life both as living laboratories for classes in botany and horticulture and as quiet, refreshing environments in a world that is becoming increasingly hectic. Few such treasured facilities can equal the Sarah P. Duke Gardens of Duke University in Durham, North Carolina. Here, in a secluded valley adjoining the campus, are fifty acres of landscaped plantings and improved forest.

The Gardens had their beginning in 1932 when Dr. Frederic Hanes of the Duke University Medical Center, which is on the campus, decided that it would be good to have a flower garden in the wooded valley near the hospital. With the financial support of Sarah P. Duke, wife of Benjamin N. Duke, a major contributor to the university, he asked John C. Wister, a Philadelphia horticulturist and landscape architect to design a small garden area featuring Dr. Hanes' favorite flower, the iris. Although the iris did not thrive here, and was confined to a small area, the garden soon became popular with students and hospital personnel alike.

In 1937, a second major area, the Terraces, was designed by Ellen Shipman of New York. The stone walk of the seven curved terraces leads several hundred feet down a gentle slope toward the woods beyond. This welcome addition was contributed by Mrs. Mary Duke Biddle in memory of her mother, Sarah P. Duke, who was so deeply involved in the Gardens' development. Mrs. Biddle's interest in the Gardens is being continued by contributions from the Mary Duke Biddle Foundation.

The Gardens later became part of the Duke University Department of Botany under the direction of Paul J. Kramer. In 1958 city planner and landscape architect William B.S. Leong was commissioned to design a master plan for Duke Gardens' orderly growth and improvement. This plan, with William Leong as consultant, is still being carried out and calls for large new areas of kept gardens while maintaining the most valuable native forest. Already completed is the Rose Garden, Azalea Court, Fern Garden and several wrought-iron screens and gates.

Duke Gardens now attracts more than 100,000 visitors a year, many of whom travel long distances to enjoy its quiet charm. The entry, near the campus, is secluded from it. Through the wrought-iron gate, designed in simple elegance by Joseph G. Barnes, there is a fine view of the distant spire of the University Chapel framed by tall trees. However, as one enters the garden, the view of the Chapel

Paul E. Genereux

The Gardens attract more than 100,000 visitors a year, many traveling long distances to enjoy their quiet charm.

Opposite: Ellen Shipman, landscape architect of New York, designed the formal terraced garden at Sarah P. Duke Gardens in 1937.

Paul E. Genereux

Since the North Carolina winters are mild, there are but a few weeks of the year when visitors cannot wander through the Gardens.

is cut off by a screen of shrubbery. This "disappearing vista" is a common European garden technique.

Along a gentle slope lined with flowers and shaded by pine trees and greenspire linden, a path leads to the Rose Garden. To the left of the path, in a forest of the finest specimens of Southern pine, a Fern Garden is currently being developed. This cool green glade with many rare ferns is financed by friends and associates of the late Dr. Hugo L. Blomquist, professor of botany at Duke University for forty-two years.

The Rose Garden, set in a circle of lawn surrounded by trees, was finished in 1963. Here one can enjoy three hundred rose bushes planted around a large, walled circle. In the center, another circular flower bed is replanted at least four times a year to present a continuous succession of colorful bloom.

To the left of the Rose Garden, a path shaded by tall hemlocks leads to the Azalea Court, another recent addition, where hundreds of bright-colored azaleas grow behind a high wall. They begin their season of bloom in early spring and some of them are in flower as late as early June.

Opposite the Azalea Court, a wisteria-covered pergola shelters a plaque in honor of Sarah P. Duke, and marks the entrance to the Terraces. The stone path, forming the axis of the seven terraces, leads from the pergola down seven flights of steps to the Water Lily Pool. The formal symmetry of the Terraces, with their fountains,

58

Placing a redbud near a cherry tree provides a striking contrast in form and texture and color.

Paul E. Genereux

The round flower bed in the center of the Rose Garden is replanted three or four times a year to provide a continuous bloom.

Courtesy Sarah P. Duke Gardens

Paul E. Genereux

Courtesy Sarah P. Duke Gardens

small pool and waterfall, is accentuated by its contrast with the surrounding informal plantings and woodlands. The top terrace is hedged in boxwood, the succeeding ones in Southern magnolia. Delicate Japanese cherry trees and flowering crab apples, alternating along the edges of the main walk, tend to soften the formality of the design. The trees planted here, as in other parts of the garden, are carefully spaced to accommodate their size as they mature. This is a lesson that most homeowners have yet to learn.

On each terrace, sweeping across the breadth of the hill, the colorful annuals and perennials create a breathtaking panorama throughout the season. The spring tulips and daffodils are followed by begonias, anemones, petunias and other popular summer flowers. Fall brings the beauty of hundreds of chrysanthemums, and in the winter the bright leaves and berries of winter jasmine, firethorn, holly and privet brighten the scene. Many plants are grown in the Gardens' propagation houses and kept there until just the time they are needed for continuous color on the Terraces.

At the base of the lower terrace is a large water lily pool fed by a waterfall from the upper terrace. The pool, with the bright accents of selected hardy water lilies, is surrounded by carefully spaced rocks and choice plants to give the area an Oriental air. Across the pool is the Rock Garden designed by the late Frederic H. Leubuscher. The view from here looking back up the Terraces reveals a bright cascade of flower colors falling from the top of the hill.

To the south of the Water Lily Pool, in sharp contrast to the formality of the Terraces, is the Earth and Sky Garden, a broad lawn with a small pool at one end. The somber green of grass and trees here meets the bright openness of North Carolina skies. To this idyllic glade professors occasionally bring their classes.

From here, as well as from other areas where the kept gardens meet the margin of the woodland, nature trails and paths wander invitingly into the woods. Tall oak trees, sweetgum, dogwood, maple and other hardwoods grow side by side with the magnificent pines that are the pride of many an informal Southern garden. In the springtime a bright carpet of naturalized narcissus blooms among the fallen pine needles and the cover of hardy ground myrtle. One of the loveliest areas is the Hanes Iris Garden, dedicated to Dr. Frederic K.M. Hanes whose interest spurred the original creation of Duke Gardens. Here, around green ovals of lawn, the irises that Dr. Hanes loved so well are planted in bright profusion. This fitting tribute is maintained by donations from grateful friends and acquaintances.

Since the North Carolina winters are mild, there are but a few weeks of the year when visitors cannot wander comfortably through the Gardens or sit and enjoy their beauty. In the winter the dark green of evergreen pines, magnolia, holly and azaleas, is brightened with berries such as holly and winter jasmine. Yet, whether in the full brilliance of summer or the quiet tones of winter, Duke Gardens fulfill their function of providing a place of rest, education and enjoyment for the students and visitors who take pleasure in the beauty of plants and flowers.

Paul E. Genereux

Above: Since 1959, when a master plan for the Gardens was prepared, the cultivated area has grown to three times its original size.

Opposite above: In expertly conceived gardens, trees are carefully spaced to accommodate their size as they mature.

Opposite below: The formal garden consists of seven curved terraces supported by dry rock walls, each approximately 150 feet long.

Asheville, North Carolina

BILTMORE HOUSE AND GARDENS

A Superb Garden Designed by Frederick Law Olmsted

One day in the mid-1880's while he sat rocking on the porch of the old Battery Park Hotel, George Vanderbilt, the grandson of Commodore Cornelius Vanderbilt, looked across the magnificent peaks of North Carolina's Blue Ridge Mountains and decided that this was the place for his country home. He had been searching for years to find a site of exceptional beauty far from the clamor of New York City. Within a few months he bought 125,000 acres of woods and hilly farm lands outside Asheville, North Carolina, naming it Biltmore after Bildt, the ancestral home of the Dutch van der Bildts and also a traditional English name for rolling countryside.

The new estate, Vanderbilt decided, should be in the style of the French Renaissance, after such historic châteaux as Chambord, Chenonceaux, and Blois. This was a considerable departure from the Georgian style so popular then in this country, but Vanderbilt, a student of architecture, was not a man to follow the crowd. His friend, Richard Morris Hunt, one of the founders and later president of the American Institute of Architects, was retained in 1890 to design a house befitting the site and pleasing the taste of his wealthy client.

Hunt proved himself equal to the job. The construction of the 250-room mansion took hundreds of workmen five years to complete. English, French, Italian, Egyptian, and native Southerners, skilled craftsmen and unskilled laborers carved and laid Indiana limestone and set into place ancient oak paneling and all the other materials hauled up the mountain on a five-mile railroad spur built especially for the Biltmore estate. When it was finished in 1895, the Biltmore mansion contained one of the largest and most opulent collections of art treasures in the United States, selected personally by George Vanderbilt on his travels around the world and shipped to Biltmore.

In the mansion's Banquet Hall, whose ceilings arch seventy-five feet over a shimmering parquet floor, the two immense thrones are classic examples of nineteenth-century Gothic wood carving. Five large tapestries, thought possibly to have been owned by King Henry VIII of England, cover the walls. The three-tiered, wrought-iron chandelier over the Grand Staircase is the largest of its kind in the world. This is but a hint of the mansion's grandeur where paintings and prints by Dürer, Renoir, John Singer Sargent, Giovanni Pellegrini, James McNeill Whistler, and other artists complement the Wedgwood furniture, soft Persian carpets and rare *objets d'art*. There are two Chinese porcelain goldfish bowls of the

Above: The four-acre Walled Garden in the English style provides an ever-blooming display in its large floral borders and beds.

Opposite: The magnificent Biltmore house in the French Renaissance style was inspired by such châteaux as Chambord and Chenonceaux.

Marble statues such as *The Dancing Lesson* accent the pools, the walks and the imposing hedges throughout the estate.

Ming Dynasty in the library and the chessmen used by Napoleon Bonaparte when he was a prisoner on St. Helena are displayed in the print room.

In the ninety-foot-long Tapestry Gallery, remarkable examples from Brussels illustrate the transition from the Gothic influence in tapestry making to that of the Renaissance. Biltmore was soon to become the favorite home of the Vanderbilt family.

To equal and complement the magnificence of the mansion the Vanderbilts hired Frederick Law Olmsted, America's leading landscape architect, to design the gardens. Olmsted, best known for his design of Central Park in New York City, created gardens at Biltmore to include thirty-five acres of formal planting, as well as many acres of more informal plantings and woodlands. From the Lodge Gate at Biltmore Village, the road winds three miles through woods and massed naturalistic plantings of rhododendron, azaleas and other flowering shrubs and trees, until, at the final turn, one views the entrance to Biltmore flanked by twin stone sphinxes.

Facing the mansion on the left, a Rampe Douce in popular Renaissance style, slopes gently up three levels to the bridle paths and glades beyond. On each level, a bronze turtle fountain stands guard. From the pergola at the top, which contains a fine statue of *Diana the Huntress*, there is an unsurpassed view of the Biltmore mansion and the surrounding countryside.

The opulence of the plantings is continued inside the mansion as well. Near the main entrance, under the high ceiling of the sunken Palm Court paved with marble, are the graceful green fronds of the palms and banks of colorful flowers which are changed with each season. In the center of the court is a fountain and sculpture of a boy with swans done by Karl Bitter, the Viennese artist who created the statues of Sculpture, Painting, Architecture, and Music in front of the Metropolitan Museum of Art in New York City. Bitter also created other designs especially for the Biltmore mansion.

The architect designed the house with the spectacular views in mind. From the Library Terrace there is a fine view of the Swimming Pool below and the formal gardens hedged in boxwood. The mountain backdrop with Mt. Pisgah looming in the distance gives the scene that aura of restfulness which George W. Vanderbilt must have felt when he first discovered the site.

Adjacent to the Library Terrace is the Italian Garden, a design of beautiful simplicity with three identical formal pools. In the first pool is the sacred lotus of Egypt; in the second, rare aquatic plants; and in the third are the bright flowers of water lilies. On the stonework of the Italian Garden is a mantle of ivy started from cuttings taken at Kenilworth Castle.

The broad stone steps lead from the Italian Garden to a large pergola, its heavy columns beautifully festooned with branches of purple wisteria. In the Shrub Garden nearby, superior specimens of Chinese holly *(Ilex cornuta)* and Japanese cut-leaf maple *(Acer palmatum dissectum)* are attractively grouped with dogwood trees, azaleas and other choice shrubs.

The four-acre Walled Garden, in the English style, is a further example of Vanderbilt's world-wide search for inspiration. Against the wall near the entrance, fruit trees are espaliered flat against the

stone surface. In the large floral borders is an ever-blooming display of popular flowers, beginning with aconites in February and proceeding with the season through daffodils, tulips, peonies and irises to a stunning show of chrysanthemums in the fall. In the typical "patterned beds" are massed displays of summer bedding plants from the Conservatory.

On the lower level of the Walled Garden is a formal Rose Garden where five thousand plants, including the old-fashioned and modern roses, are combined in colorful harmony. Twining on wires and iron posts are several rare examples of the climbers developed around the turn of the century by M.H. Walsh of Woods Hole, Massachusetts. In 1957, part of the Rose Garden was converted to use as an All-America Rose Test Garden so that now the best of the modern hybrids can be seen here.

The Conservatory and greenhouses, at the far end of the Walled Garden, were completely rebuilt in 1957 according to their original plan. This is a working area where plants are grown for display in the patterned beds and Palm Court and as cut flowers for the mansion. These greenhouses also supply the Biltmore Nurseries, near the Gardens' exit gate, where visitors and residents of the Asheville area can purchase plants and flowers of excellent quality.

Against the wall near the entrance to the Walled Garden, fruit trees are espaliered flat against the stone surface.

Although they seem original, the hardwood and conifer forests surrounding the estate were planted when the garden was established.

Opposite: To complement the magnificence of the mansion, the Vanderbilts hired Frederick Law Olmsted, America's first landscape architect, to design the gardens.

Beyond the formal plantings lies the informal Azalea Garden, the work of the late Chauncy Beadle, a Canadian horticulturist hired to carry out Olmsted's garden plans and who stayed to supervise the Gardens for some sixty years. Mr. Beadle was an azalea enthusiast and on trips throughout the United States he sought out the best and added them to his own private collection. In 1949 this floral treasure was donated to the Biltmore Gardens and planted among the tall pines in what was originally the Pinetum. Here, among the trees and clipped grass, the Azalea Garden slopes gently toward the Bass Pond where a rustic bridge crosses a stream near a sparkling waterfall. The planting is considered to be the largest and most complete collection of native American azaleas in the world. These American azaleas, along with some of their choice Asian counterparts, create a stunning springtime show in the hills of Biltmore.

Beyond the azalea plantings are the lovely wooded hills of the Blue Ridge. The luxuriant hardwood and conifer forests immediately around the estate give the impression of native growth. They were, however, planted for the most part when the gardens were being established. The land that Mr. Vanderbilt purchased east of the French Broad River had been worked out and was badly eroded. Forestry was one of his hobbies so he hired Gifford Pinchot, one of the first trained foresters in the United States (later Governor of Pennsylvania), to plant the entire area. Dr. C.A. Schenck, of the University of Darmstadt in Germany, was hired to supervise the work. Through the talents of these two men, new methods in forestry were developed and the reforestation was dramatically successful. Many of the techniques they practiced here are helping today to preserve our forest lands. J. Sterling Morton, Secretary of Agriculture at the time, once said that Vanderbilt put more money into this one forestry project than was available to finance the entire Department of Agriculture.

In 1898, Dr. Schenck established the Biltmore School of Forestry, the first such facility in the United States. Though the school was disbanded with the advent of World War I, many of the men who dominated the field during the past century got their training here.

After George Vanderbilt's death in 1914, his wife Edith Vanderbilt donated some thirty thousand acres of land in the Mt. Pisgah area to the United States Government. This was the nucleus for the Mt. Pisgah National Forest which now includes part of the famous Blue Ridge Parkway. Forestry students still come here to study the work begun by Pinchot and Schenck.

Biltmore became the permanent home of the Vanderbilt's daughter Cornelia after her marriage to John Francis Amherst Cecil, and it was she who opened the estate to the public in 1930. It is now owned and operated by Vanderbilt's grandsons through the Biltmore Company.

There are not many gardens where one can see styles and plantings of such variety so effectively integrated by the discipline of the overall design.

Right: By early spring, plants that have been stirring since February suddenly burst into a profusion of color and fragrance.

Opposite: The informal Azalea Garden is the work of Chauncey Beadle, a Canadian horticulturist who donated his private azalea collection to the Gardens in 1949.

Below: The Conservatory and greenhouses, rebuilt in 1957 according to the original plan, supply cut flowers for the mansion.

REYNOLDA GARDENS

A Place of Contemplation and Research

Originally composed of a four-acre formal garden, Reynolda Gardens now envelops more than one hundred acres.

Opposite: Leading from a group of stately Japanese cedars in the center of the garden to the Conservatory and greenhouses is a broad avenue of Cryptomeria.

A grant, from the Mary Reynolds Babcock Foundation to Wake Forest University, of four acres of formal gardens on the former estate of R.J. Reynolds marked the beginning of Reynolda Gardens in 1958. The deed read in part: "There is an evergrowing need (in Forsyth County) for land areas to be set aside, preserved and enhanced in the beauty of their natural state, which land area can become a refuge for relaxation and contemplation and a haven for reflective leisure of all mankind."

In the Formal Gardens, adjacent to the Wake Forest University campus, visitors can find such beautiful flowers as tree and shrub peonies, wisteria, and roses growing sedately behind clipped boxwood hedges in carefully tailored rectangular beds. Borders of *Liriope* and paving-stone walks surround the grassy plots and flower beds. The delicate cascades of the Japanese weeping cherries are protected by a row of saucer magnolias *(M. soulangeana)*.

The Gardens were designed early in the 1920's by Thomas W. Sears, a Philadelphia landscape architect. It is on his excellent original plans that the later additions have been based. In the center of the garden stands a group of stately Japanese cedars *(Cryptomeria japonica)*. A broad Cryptomeria Avenue leads from here to the Conservatory and greenhouses. At one end of the avenue, several small open garden houses, reminiscent of Japanese pagodas, shelter the inviting chairs and tables.

Ranged around the high Central Conservatory, which opens into the Formal Gardens, are the greenhouses. These are of the utmost importance to Reynolda for horticultural research. Formerly carried out by individuals, this research has increasingly become the province of the University staff. In two of the large greenhouses, plant propagation and research projects are developed, both for the Gardens and for the University. The other greenhouses are used in cooperation with commercial florists.

As Reynolda Gardens has become a vital part of the life of the University and nearby communities, it has continued to grow since its founding a little over a decade ago. At first there was only the four acres of Formal Gardens. Subsequent gifts of adjacent land have resulted in the garden's growth to its present size of more than one hundred acres. Most of this is natural woodlands which now make up about sixty percent of the total area. Laced with streams and with occasional ponds, the woodlands are a beautiful environmental foil to the formal and research areas.

A number of small open garden houses, reminiscent of Japanese pagodas, are placed invitingly throughout the Formal Gardens.

The native dogwoods to be found in the woodlands along the nature trails of Reynolda Gardens are unexcelled.

Silas Creek, which runs through the property, was dammed about fifty years ago to form Lake Katherine. The lake originally covered about eleven acres, but due to extensive silting, it has considerably decreased in size and the silted areas have given rise to several acres of cattails. Their stout stalks and reed-like foliage grow thickly together providing cover and food for migrating geese and other water fowl. The lake and adjacent wetlands offer several interesting biological environments which are valuable for education and research. There are plans to do some dredging here and to create an island. Weeping cherry and willow trees will then be planted on the banks of both the island and the lake.

Below the dam, which forms Lake Katherine, a waterfall plummets into a quiet pool surrounded by steep banks and woods. The original walks of rough granite stone, in combination with the peacefulness of the woodland, make a pleasant and picturesque retreat for university students and visiting nature lovers. Azaleas, planned for planting on the steep banks of the pool, will add a colorful accent to this lovely area. One of the tributaries of the lake, a "run" or small creek, forms a shallow ravine in which several species of fern grow beautifully. A path follows along the ravine where interesting plants have been introduced, including the rare Shortia *(S. galacifolia)* and the erect stalks of *equisetum*, or horsetail, whose ancestors covered much of the earth some 300 million years ago during the Mesozoic period.

Here as elsewhere along the nature trails, most of the native shrubs and trees have been labeled for easy identification with both the common and botanical names. In some cases the family name is added to the back of the label for the information of botanists.

The native dogwoods *(Cornus florida)* to be found in the woodlands and along the trails of Reynolda Gardens are unexcelled. They are large of trunk, the foliage is rich and full and they flower in great profusion. Seven different species of oak *(Quercus)* and five species of hickory *(Carya)* are present. Other native species of special interest and beauty are the sourwood *(Oxydendrum arboreum)*, the native redbud *(Cercis)*, tall stately tulip trees *Liriodendron)*, the yellow pine with its bark divided into segments like armored plate, American holly, and the Virginia persimmon.

Plantings of hollies, grouped according to geographic origin, are arranged along the trails. For any gardener particularly interested in holly, this alone makes a visit to Reynolda worthwhile. To be seen here is the European holly *(Ilex aquifolium)* as well as *I. altaclarensis* and other varieties. Native hollies include the inkberry *(Ilex glabra)*, the American holly *(I. opaca)*, together with its varieties Croonenberg, East Palatka and *fosteri*. There is the black alder holly *(I. verticillata)*, the yaupon *(I. vomitoria)* and two of the dwarf kinds. The Chinese hollies represented are *I. ciliospinosa, I. cornuta burfordi, I. cornuta* dwarf, *I. pedunclosa* and *I. pernyi*. The present Japanese holly collection is made up of *I. latifolia* plants and of representatives of *I. crenata* and a number of its varieties

Above: Streams and an occasional pond lace the natural woodlands which make up about sixty percent of the Gardens.

Below: Old boxwood hedges and extensive *Liriope* borders are among the features of the Formal Gardens designed by Thomas W. Sears.

including compacta, convexa, fastigiata, Helleri, Maxwell, machrophylla, nigra, repandens and willow leaf. All in all, it is an impressive collection of this handsome genus.

Much of the land recently acquired for Reynolda will be improved in the coming years. One of the most comprehensive plans concerns a rather flat, grassy expanse of about thirty acres which makes up the eastward extension of the Gardens. Known as the "Big Green," it is bordered by fairly dense woods on one side and by scattered native trees, and some exotic plants, on the other. Various trees and shrubs will be planted here as an extension of the woodland areas which are already a natural arboretum. These added plants will be placed in proper botanical relationships as well as for the overall landscape effect. A beginning has been made here by placing a number of ginkgo trees, as well as such shrubs and small trees as crab apple, fringe-tree, mountain ash and rhododendron — which grows to near tree-size here.

Many other exotic plants are already found on the lawns near the nature trails, including many mature specimens of deodar cedars, a large bald cypress, smoke tree *(Cotinus coggygria)*, Phoenix tree *(Firmiana simplex)*, weeping willows and long leafed pine. The Chinese dogwood *(Cornus kousa)* is included for its magnificent white flowers that cover the tree several weeks after the native dogwood bloom is past. The "flowers" (botanically speaking, they are bracts) are more pointed than the native dogwood.

Reynolda House is surrounded by the Gardens, although it's not officially a part of them. Originally called "The Bungalow," it was designed by Charles Barton Keene of Philadelphia for Richard Joshua Reynolds. Completed in 1917, three generations of the family lived here over a period of fifty years. Reynolda House, Incorporated, now maintains and preserves the house, its furnishings and an interesting collection of art for the enjoyment of the public.

The Winston-Salem Nature-Science Center, founded in 1964, though not a part of the Gardens themselves, is housed in buildings belonging to Wake Forest University and is immediately adjacent to the Gardens. The Science Center supplements the work of Reynolda Gardens in serving the University and the community by providing useful information about the animals, the plants, the rocks and other natural features of North Carolina.

Walter S. Flory, Director of Reynolda Gardens and holder of the Babcock Chair in botany at Wake Forest University, lists the three major goals of a botanical garden in a present day university: To further basic research. To aid university teaching. To render public service, especially to the constituents of the area.

The Formal Gardens, greenhouses, forest lands and Nature-Science Center have combined to fulfill and extend to an admirable degree the goals defined by Mr. Flory as well as the stated purpose of the original grant — to provide a place for "relaxation and contemplation" and, one might add, for furthering the frontiers of horticultural science. There is a climate developing here in which ideas as well as plants will thrive.

Courtesy Reynolda Gardens

The formality of boxwood hedges is offset
by Japanese flowering cherries and magnolias.

CALLAWAY GARDENS

A Garden of Unusual Diversity

A woodland garden and wildlife sanctuary, Callaway is located 1,300 feet above sea level on the slopes of Pine Mountain, Georgia.

Opposite: The shore of each of the twelve lakes at Callaway Gardens is planted with its own flower specialty.

Callaway Gardens, located 1,300 feet above sea level on the wooded slopes of Pine Mountain, Georgia, is a place of unusual diversity. In addition to being a woodland garden and sanctuary for thousands of Appalachian wildflowers, the Gardens are a year-round playground with twelve lakes, boating and fishing, sixty-three holes of golf, a thousand-acre quail preserve, horseback riding and a circus.

The Gardens began in the 1940's as the private project of Cason Callaway, owner of Georgia's Callaway Mills. They are now owned and operated, on a non-profit basis, by the Callaway's second son, Howard "Bo" Callaway.

In the early 1930's, Bo Callaway remembers, his father and mother drove out to Pine Mountain looking for a picnic spot for the family. Pine Mountain, at the southern end of the Appalachian chain, includes some of the oldest land on the American continent, having evolved to its present form even before the Rockies pushed their way up through the prehistoric sea that once covered this country. Most of this foothill land was eroded and overworked by generations of settlers attempting to eke out an existence. The trees were felled, the land burned over and deserted. In a few valleys, too steep to farm, the original trees and grasses still grew, watered by mountain springs and streams. It was one of these secluded spots that the Callaways found.

"When the telephone began to ring all day Sunday," Cason Callaway said, "I knew it was time to find a place where I could just walk in the woods and look at the beauty that God had made and think about things I hadn't had time to think about before." One spring day, while wandering in the woods, Cason Callaway discovered an unfamiliar flower growing near the Barnes Creek watershed of Blue Springs. He took it home to his wife, Virginia, who identified it as a *Rhododendron prunifolium azalea,* a flower so rare that it grows nowhere else on earth except within a hundred mile radius of Blue Springs. In order to preserve and maintain the unique azalea, the Callaways bought three thousand acres of land at Blue Springs on Pine Mountain and built a log house there for summer vacationing.

At about this time, Governor Richard B. Russell asked Cason Callaway to serve on the Board of Regents of the University of Georgia. Callaway, busy with his work at the mills, had paid little attention to the problems of education since his own student days at the University of Virginia. He was appalled at the small amount of

Maintenance is so thorough that even the woodland flowers are watered weekly with an inch of "rainfall" from a portable pump.

Opposite: Easily accessible by car, the Woodlands are planted with rare and common wildflowers such as trilliums, tiny bluets, wild hydrangeas and grass of Parnassus.

money allotted to the state universities. On further examination, however, Callaway learned that Georgia actually put a higher percentage of its income into school support than many other states. So he decided that the best way to get more money for schools was to raise the average income of the state.

Since farming was a major source of state income, Callaway developed Blue Springs Farm for experimental purposes on Pine Mountain. He moved his family to the log house at Blue Springs, near the "Little White House" of his close friend and neighbor, Franklin D. Roosevelt. Here he grew blueberries, scuppernongs, white African guineas, geese, pheasants, Mallard ducks and Cornish game hens. He experimented with hybrid pine trees that grew thirty-five percent faster than the old-fashioned pines. In the streams, which he dammed into ponds, he grew fish as a game crop. The Blue Springs Farm became a nationally famous experimental station for new methods in agriculture and conservation.

Callaway realized that the small farmer would need cash to raise such crops, so he became an apostle of long-term loans for farmers.

In 1938, at the age of forty-four, Cason Callaway resigned from the La Grange Mills to devote his life to Blue Springs Farm. As the farm prospered, the ever-busy Callaway looked for new places to expand. With the men and machines available to him he set out to dam the creek on the western part of his property to make eleven lakes ranging in size from 175 acres to small ponds. Around the lakes a nine-hole golf course was built.

At first Cason Callaway thought of creating a great estate where he could someday build a home and where his retired friends from the business world could build houses and spend their time playing golf and bridge. Looking at his handiwork, however, he thought of his mother Ida Callaway, and his wife Virginia; and resolved that, as a tribute to them, something more meaningful would be done with this beautiful land. He resolved to open the farm with all its improvements to the public as a place of recreation and as a shelter for the shrubs, trees, flowers, birds, and animals he and his wife loved so well.

Cason Callaway explained to one visitor: "What I'm trying to do here is hang the picture a little higher on the wall for the people of this region. Every child ought to see something beautiful before he's six years old — something he will remember all his life. And there hasn't been too much beauty in this part of the country in the past . . . . I don't know what the soul is, but whatever it is, a sense of beauty and goodness must be at the heart of it."

The change from private preserve to a public garden required new planning which Mr. Callaway went into with typical thoroughness and enthusiasm. Out on U.S. Route 27 which goes by the gardens, he planted great masses of long-blooming pink roses between the lanes of the highway. For his new guests he planned a sandy beach. Nineteen thousand tons of sand were brought to the gardens and laid in a 2,800-foot shelf around sixty-five-acre Lake Robin. Nature trails were laid out all through the woods.

In early April, before the leaves have formed on the tall oaks and maples, the woods are colored pink and white by azaleas and dogwood.

Both Mr. and Mrs. Callaway were most interested in the horticultural aspects of the garden. To prepare themselves for the task of transplanting and growing Appalachian wildflowers, the two of them spent some time at Cornell University studying horticulture and botany. Then, with the help of a fifty-man gardening staff, they began the job of landscaping the 2,500-acre garden.

The shore of each lake on the estate is planted with its own flower specialty. At Bobolink, flame azaleas glow brightly against the green woods. Dogwood and wild pink azaleas bloom around Bluebird Lake. At Hummingbird, the scent of hundreds of magnolias perfumes the air. At Mockingbird and Whippoorwill, crab apples and hydrangeas provide a blaze of color. Each year twenty thousand new plants are set out in the woods around the lakes. Many of these come from Pine Mountain itself, and are grown and propagated in the Gardens' own greenhouses and lath houses. In the Woodlands, easily accessible by car, rare and common wildflowers were planted for the pleasure of city dwellers who could seldom see such a collection. Here are wild hydrangeas, gordonias, trilliums, wild roses, blue gentians, tiny bluets, sweet shrub, redbud, grass of Parnassus; and such rare plants as *Magnolia cordata*, with its canary-yellow flower, and the plum-leaf azalea *(R. prunifolium azalea)* which planted the first seed of a garden idea in Mr. Callaway's imagination. Although their personal interest was mainly in the plants and flowers, the Callaways did not neglect the recreational facilities for the new garden-playground. In 1952 the Ida Cason Callaway Gardens, named after Mr. Callaway's mother, were opened to the public.

In 1953 the Callaway's son "Bo" returned from college at West Point, and from the Korean War. He found his father excited over the scores of visitors now making their way to the garden. "I'm a selfish man at heart," Cason Callaway told his son. "I want to use my money to do people good and make them happy while I'm still alive to watch and enjoy it." Mr. Callaway was full of plans for expanding the Gardens: a quiet chapel in the woods, new flowers and plants, cottages where families from La Grange and Atlanta and other towns nearby could come to spend their vacations. The Callaways, father and son, worked together on the Gardens and shortly afterwards, Cason Callaway turned them over to his son, retaining only what he called "meddling privileges." By the time Mr. Callaway died in 1961 most of the projects he visualized were well on their way to completion.

Today, under the management of Bo Callaway, the Callaway Gardens, so young compared to most of America's major gardens, are famous in horticultural circles. In the forest and around the large, quiet lakes, the nature trails are an ever-changing source of delight. Four hundred varieties of holly are displayed along five holly trails — one trail of Japanese hollies *(Ilex crenata)*, one of the English species *(I. aquifolium)*, and three of the American *(I. opaca)*.

The Laurel Springs Trail reveals the essence of an Appalachian hardwood forest. In early April, before the leaves have formed on the tall oaks and maples along the trail, the woods are pink and white with the blossoms of mountain laurel, Piedmont azalea and dogwood. Through the summer there are the blossoms and fruits of such berries as sparkleberry, chokeberry, Southern wax-myrtle, huckleberry and elderberry. The flowers of the pink and white oakleaf hydrangea brighten the shady woodland. Along the cool, moist edge of the stream are the swamp plants and elegant fronds of such ferns as the royal chain and cinnamon. The evergreen Christmas fern and lady ferns are abundant in this area and throughout the Gardens. In the fall, for a dramatic end-of-season show, the bright leaves of the hardwood trees blend their colors with the soft red of sumac and the red of winter berries.

Over three hundred varieties of azaleas grow along Azalea Trail which starts from the club house parking area and winds its way toward the Horticulture Office. Another wildflower trail, the Chapel

Through the summer, green lilies and blue water set off blossoms and fruits of such berries as sparkleberry and chokeberry.

In the forest and around the lakes, the nature trails are an ever-changing source of delight. The Gardens contain five holly trails.

Opposite: Each year twenty thousand new plants are set out in the woods around the lakes. Many are grown in the Gardens' greenhouses.

Trail, covers the area around Rocky Falls Lake, keeping almost constantly in view the natural fieldstone chapel which Cason Callaway had built in the woods in memory of his mother. For those who prefer to drive instead of walk, a five-mile scenic drive meanders through the woods.

The needs of the plants here in their natural habitat are as carefully considered as in any formal garden or greenhouse. The old garden axiom that it is better to put a dollar plant in a five-dollar hole than a five-dollar plant in a one-dollar hole is faithfully practiced here. The maintenance is so thorough that even the woodland flowers are watered weekly with an inch of "rainfall" from a portable pump.

A Bird Study Trail has been planted with trees and shrubs to attract and sustain the scores of birds which make their home in the gardens. And in 1955 the Callaway Gardens were officially recognized as a bird sanctuary.

Bo Callaway has recently completed the group of cottages his father had planned just before his death. There are now 155 cottages skillfully blended into a grove of pine woods and designed so families can vacation here comfortably and inexpensively.

An important and impressive planting here is the seven-and-a-half acres of fruits, vegetables, and berries known as Mr. Cason's Garden. It was developed as a demonstration garden for visitors interested in better ways to grow their own fruits and vegetables, and it also provides delicious food for the Club House dining rooms.

In respect to Cason Callaway's wishes, there has been no attempt to bring such mechanical devices as pinball machines into the resort. He preferred the pleasures of a barge which takes visitors on a five-mile trip around Robin Lake, or paddleboats for those who wish to go off alone. Months of persuasion were necessary to obtain his agreement to the addition of a miniature train which tours the edge of Lake Chickadee.

For those who prefer spectator sports, daily shows from June through Labor Day feature expert water skiers and a unique kite flying act. The Florida State University Circus regularly spends the summer at Callaway Gardens and presents several shows a week.

The thirty members of the circus troupe, all college students, also plan and supervise a recreation program including water skiing, group games, nature lore, and other subjects for the youngsters who vacation at Callaway Gardens. The Callaways were always fond of children. Another of the programs envisioned by Cason Callaway is now being carried out. This is a plan to give special recognition to outstanding high school students. The students, chosen by twenty to thirty youth organizations in Georgia, are given a week's free vacation with their families at the Gardens.

Cason Callaway was a man with a vision the breadth and scope of which are revealed by the gardens he created. "The gardens," says the son who carries on his work, "tell the story of a man, and his dream. . . . Go see for yourself. All their gates are open."

Cypress Gardens, Florida

CYPRESS GARDENS

A Splendid Dream Brought to Reality in Central Florida

J. Johnson

There are one and a half miles of waterways through the Gardens and over a mile of intriguing pathways.

Opposite: Bald cypresses draped with hanging Spanish moss are the outstanding feature at Cypress Gardens. Some are 1,800 years old.

Cypress Gardens, located five miles southeast of Winter Haven in central Florida, is something of a miracle in more ways than one. It is first a miracle of color created by bright azaleas, green lawns, sparkling lagoons and tall palm trees. It is also a miracle of engineering. Nearly half the garden was dredged out of a Florida swamp by an amazing horticultural businessman, Dick Pope, whom local residents once scoffingly called the Swami of the Swamp.

It all started in 1931 when Pope, then a prosperous publicity man, moved to Florida from his native state of Iowa. Becoming a member of the Lake Region Canal Commission he persuaded this group, which was already at work building channels to connect the eighteen lakes within five miles of Winter Haven, to put up $2,800 toward developing a dozen acres of swamp on the shores of Lake Eloise. They loaned him the money, but when the local people became skeptical of the idea of draining the swamp, the commission gave the idea up as a fool's project and demanded the money back. Pope, who first intended to take prospective real estate customers for boat rides, had struck upon the idea of making the property into a garden. He paid back the Canal Commission, hired forty men at one dollar per day each and began building his garden as a private project, increasing its size year by year until it reached its present large proportions.

Cypress Gardens opened in 1936. Two years later there were ten electric boats for scenic rides through the meandering waterways under the tall cypress trees which first attracted the attention of the garden's founder. Cypress Gardens began to prosper.

Before starting his garden venture the gregarious Dick Pope had the experience of a career that was equally venturesome. He and his brother Malcolm were first famous as stunt men in Florida. Malcolm was the first man ever to jump over obstacles in a boat, and Dick the first to jump on water skis. In 1929 they wired forty-eight skyrockets to their boat and set them off. The boat got up to fifty-eight miles per hour.

Pope was selling real estate in Florida in the mid-1920's when the big real estate crash came. When he heard that Johnson Motors of Waukegan, Illinois, was about to launch a big publicity campaign

Spanish moss is not a parasite, but an air plant. It is used to make plastics, penicillin molds and cattle feed.

Opposite: Amid the flowers, lending the impression of Southern elegance, girls dressed in antebellum costume act as hostesses.

Photos: Courtesy Cypress Gardens

for its outboard motors, he started to drive to Waukegan stopping at every major city along the way to wire the company's president: "Hold all publicity plans until I get there. Your problem is solved." Pope got the job.

For all their beauty, the Gardens posed something of a publicity challenge. They were located more than four miles from the nearest main highway and miles from any major city. Imaginative promotion was needed to encourage the public to seek out its isolated swampland site. Pope proved himself more than equal to the situation. Seven full-time photographers sent out hundreds of photographs. Bumper stickers were pasted on every car that came into the Gardens' big parking lot. Pope created Florida's first flower queen contest. The most beautiful places in the garden were offered to business and advertising agencies as ideal for shooting their advertising photographs. Once only a government order prevented the ebullient Pope from throwing a million gardenias off the top of the Empire State Building as an advertising gimmick. But the ballyhoo paid off. More than one and a half million people from the United States and all parts of the world visit these beautiful grounds every year.

Pope planned the landscaping himself, using a camera viewfinder to establish what would later become a photographer's paradise. When he started Cypress Gardens in 1936 he knew almost nothing about flowers. Once, discovering that he didn't know how to spell azalea, he advised his secretary to call the plant "flame vine." Now, however, Dick Pope is as expert on the 2,200 different species of plants that grow in his garden as any of his staff of thirty-five gardeners. Under the supervision of Chief Horticulturist Paul Rutter, the gardeners here pay close attention to the horticultural details of exposure to sun and shade, soil structure, watering, fertilizing, cold protection and control of insects and fungi.

One of the Gardens' outstanding features is, of course, the abundance of cypress trees. Only one species, the bald cypress *(Taxodium distichum)*, is found here. These trees range in age from 150 to 1,800 years and are native to the region. They grow only about an inch and a half at the base every forty-six years. Hanging eerily from the branches of the cypress are clouds of Spanish moss *(Tillandsia usneoides)*. It is not a parasite, but an air plant closely related to the pineapple. It is used commercially in the making of cattle feed, plastics, penicillin molds and as a base for cosmetics.

With the stately cypress, the great variety of flowers and other plants, Cypress Gardens seems to grow steadily in beauty each year. Today, the garden features banks of azaleas in stunning shades of red, pink and orange. Along the miles of paths meandering through the Gardens and along the banks of the dark canals, there are plantings of camellias, red and purple bougainvillea, chrysanthemums and dozens of hibiscus. Gardenias, flourishing in the rich dark soil, often grow to a size of more than six feet, and spread their heady perfume throughout the Gardens.

Along the canals, where bridges made of cypress arch over the mirror-like waters, there are countless interesting tropical plants which flourish year-round in Florida's temperate climate. Exotic orchids, birds-of-paradise, Amazon and ginger lilies grow profusely throughout the Gardens. There are fifty-five varieties of palm trees including the unusual pygmy date palm *(Phoenix roebeleni)* from China; the fish-tail palm *(Caryota mitis)* from Burma and Malaya; and the royal palm *(Roystonea regia)*, a native of southern Florida, which reaches heights of nearly a hundred feet. Papyrus *(Cyperus papyrus)* from Egypt, Australian cajeput trees *(Meleleuca leucadendra)*, the traveler's-tree *(Ravenala madagascariensis)* from Madagascar and several unusual South American jungle plants also grow here, along with the more common varieties of American trees and the holly, bay, gordonia and wax myrtles of the American South.

Among the unusual plants to be seen here are the giant water lily *(Victoria regia)*, a six-foot-wide floating lily with up-turned red edges, the Chinese rice paper plant *(Tetrapanax papyriferum)*, the bark of which was used as a painting material centuries ago by Chinese artists; and garland flower *(Hedychium coronarium)*, which has a white crown and yellow throat and is used in Hawaii for making leis. Other plants of special interest include the royal princess or glory tree *(Tibouchina granulosa)*, which blooms eight months of the year and seldom grows much north of Orlando, Florida. Here, too, can be seen the pandorea *(Tecoma ricasoliana)*, one of the most beautiful flowering vines of the semi-tropics; corkscrew ginger *(Costus igneus)*, a tropical plant with red cone buds; and hunter's robe *(Pothos aureus)*, a climbing vine from the Solomon Islands, used by hunting natives as a camouflage.

Other plants growing in Cypress Gardens, seldom found elsewhere in the United States, are the green and white striped bananas, the Star of India bougainvillea that has red and white flowers on the same plant, several species of Tibouchina (unnamed at present) and a white jacaranda tree.

In addition, there is a rose garden featuring Florida roses, a Japanese garden, a Mexican cactus garden and a rock garden near a small waterfall. Secluded lagoons add to the peaceful beauty. Amid the flowers, lending the impression of Southern elegance, girls dressed in antebellum costume act as hostesses.

There is more at Cypress Gardens than floral and feminine beauty — especially for those interested in water sports. On the lake four times a day the Garden presents its world-famous ski show that, like the garden itself, had a humble beginning. In August of 1942, during World War II, six soldiers arrived from a nearby army camp. "When does the show start?" one of the group asked Mrs. Pope. There was no show, but Mrs. Pope replied, "A little after three o'clock." Then she sent a secretary to Winter Haven High School to round up Dick Pope, Jr., his sister Adrienne and four other teenagers. The kids, all water-skiing enthusiasts, improvised a

One of the special sections of the Gardens is the South Sea Waterfall, a luxuriant tropical retreat.

Opposite: Flaming bright red salvia lines the banks of this canal and a bridge made of cypress spans the dark water.

David W. Corson from A. Devaney, N.Y.

A versatile flower, the azalea can be used in hedges and for screening, as border or foundation plantings.

"show," and it was a hit. The next weekend a convoy of eight hundred soldiers arrived at the Gardens, and the ski show has been part of the Cypress Gardens program ever since.

Supervising all the activities is Dick Pope, a ruddy-cheeked man of five-feet-five whose typical costume is a Hawaiian print shirt, buff slacks, a brass-buttoned blazer, brown and white perforated alligator-hide shoes and a braided yachting cap. With undying optimism he claims that weather reports should give "mostly sunny" instead of "partly cloudy." And when it rains he says, "It's the best lousy weather in the country." He is so involved with the garden that he had his office built without windows to avoid distractions, but it soon became so infinitely frustrating not to be able to see what was going on outside that he relented and had a periscope installed through the office roof.

Since the Gardens began in 1936 the Popes have played host to royalty, to presidents, to movie and television stars, as well as beauty-lovers from far and wide. The Gardens have appeared in numerous television shows: *The Mike Douglas Show, The Arthur Godfrey Show, What's My Line?* and *The Ed Sullivan Show*, as well as a special about the Gardens starring Johnny Carson and in feature-length Hollywood movies, two starring Esther Williams and one in

Cinerama. The Florida-shaped pool that Esther Williams used in the movie "Easy to Love" is still one of the Gardens' features.

The Gardens are now run by the Popes' son, Dick, Jr., who is President of the Florida Cypress Gardens. Dick Jr., who was the first to succeed at barefoot water skiing, is married to one of the Gardens' former Citrus Queens, Frances Layton. They were married before the end of her reign, and it was necessary for the young Mrs. Pope to give up her crown. When the Duke of Windsor met the couple, he laughingly told Pope, "That makes your wife and myself members of the smallest club in the world."

Under the direction of the second generation, the work of the Gardens goes on. New flowers are added regularly and Cypress develops its own hybrids. Over 260 palm trees with an average height of thirty feet were transplanted in and around the garden in a six-month period to enhance its tropical character. Most of the great gardens are the result of one man's dream. Few are the places that have attained the beauty and acclaim of Cypress Gardens against such overwhelming odds.

Right: To enhance the Gardens' tropical nature,
over 260 palm trees of various species
were transplanted in a six-month period.

Below: Holding a pointed shovel in one hand and
an open Bible in the other is St. Fiacre,
Patron Saint of Gardeners.

Photos Courtesy Cypress Gardens

Tampa, Florida

BUSCH GARDENS

A Tropical Wildlife Sanctuary

In the lagoons, which are stocked with goldfish, ducks of all varieties, geese, cranes, ibis and swans make their homes.

Opposite: A geodesic dome ninety-nine feet in diameter and made of gold anodized aluminum houses the Gardens' more exotic birds.

One of the country's most modern and ingenious garden installations is Busch Gardens, adjoining the Anheuser-Busch Brewery in Tampa, Florida. Not only are there two hundred species of flowers on display and some 150,000 trees and shrubs, but such innovations as a monorail, an outstanding geodesic dome, and one of the largest collections of rare and domestic birds in the United States, as well as a fine collection of wild animals.

In 1959, August A. Busch, Jr., started building the Tampa brewery on thirty-five acres of industrial park located eight miles north of downtown Tampa. The Gardens were his idea for an experiment in community relations. Fifteen acres of the sandy slope next to the brewery were transformed into a lush tropical garden, replete with wide lawns, tall palm trees and three connecting lagoons. The experiment has proved to be a thorough success. The Gardens, with two to three million visitors each year, have become Florida's number one tourist attraction — so successful, in fact, that recently a 186-acre wildlife sanctuary was added.

The tour of Busch Gardens begins at the eighty-six-foot escalator that carries passengers up to an observation deck on the roof of the Lager Cellers Building. From here the visitor gets a "parrot's eye" view of the Gardens with its lagoons and hundreds of birds, the Wild Animal Kingdom, the industrial park and the nearby University of South Florida. Below, in a tiled pool, playful sea lions splash about and take the Florida sun.

Next there is a stop at the Gardens' focal point, the heptagonal-roofed Hospitality House. The roof seems to float over this unusual structure overlooking one of the Gardens' three lagoons. There is a broad observation deck, cantilevered out over the lagoon, where white swans swim in the sparkling blue waters. The flowers at the Gardens provide a brilliant accent for the lush green of the trees and shrubbery. Thousands of marigolds line the entranceway and red salvia, petunias, gardenias and camellias are beautifully displayed in massed plantings. Each fall some 100,000 annuals are set out for a bright panorama of color from January to December.

There is color to be seen on every side. But, in addition to the floral displays, the Gardens abound with other fascinating horticultural specimens, as well. Not surprisingly in this semi-tropical climate, Busch Gardens has several fine species of palms. Here one

Peafowl make up a part of the hundreds of birds which comprise one of the largest avian displays in the world.

can see the familiar everglade palm of Florida and the date palm, which the Arabs cultivated in the arid regions of the Old World. One specie, however, is quite unusual. In fact, of the 150,000 trees and shrubs found at the Gardens, the rarest is the unique Senegal Palm from Africa *(Phoenix reclinata)*. Sixty years ago a Tampa doctor's wife brought the seed for this tree from Spain. It was originally planted in nearby Ybor City, but its spread of some sixty feet soon stood in the way of industrial expansion. So that it could be moved by truck, it had to be cut into five pieces. Now, reassembled in Busch Gardens, its trunk configuration of complete circles, resembling the coils of a snake, is believed to be unique.

Less rare but equally fascinating is the giant reed *(Arundo donax)* which grows profusely throughout the Gardens. It is the tallest of the ornamental grasses, often reaching heights of twenty feet, and is planted for the bold effects of its long, drooping, bright green leaves and its showy reddish brown plumes — occasionally more than a foot long.

Against the prevailing greenery of the Gardens, two colorful flowering shrubs stand out: the natal-plum from South Africa *(Carissa grandiflora)* and the Australian bottle-brush *(Callistemon)*.

The natal-plum has a wealth of white or pink pinwheel flowers with heavy perfume, and is named for the glossy red fruit that follows the flowers. It has dark thick leaves and heavy spines. The Australian bottle-brush, rather frequently grown in Florida, produces long slender leaves and, at the tips of the twigs, myriad small cream-white to red flowers in cylindrical masses — with the appearance of a bottle brush.

Of the many herbs which grow here perhaps the most striking is the alstroemeria, a large genus of the amaryllis family. It is a South American herb with leafy stems and showy red, yellow or purple flowers. The more familiar plants range from flowers, such as the day lily and bird-of-paradise, to grasses such as bamboo or bambusa, and the acacia, a tree and shrub that grows primarily in the tropics, particularly Australia.

A Florida garden without the citrus fruits for which the state is famous would be unthinkable, so Busch Gardens has included the calamondin *(Citrus mitis)* and the kumquat in its colorful array of plantings. The calamondin is unique among the citrus as the hardiest of the species now grown in America. With its graceful shape, bright green leaves and small, tangerine-like fruits it is also one of the most ornamental of all the citrus. The juice of the calamondin is extremely acid, but it has a good flavor and is excellent as a base for fruit punch. The kumquat has the distinction of being the smallest plant and the smallest fruit of the citrus in cultivation in America. It is commonly grown as a shrub, the largest reaching a height of twelve feet and a diameter of about eight feet.

In one corner of the garden is a Dwarf Village designed to delight children of all ages. Here, in a forest setting with rhododendron shading the tiny houses, is Butterfly Gap, Old Whiskers Glen, Leprechaun Lane, and such famous storybook characters as Hansel and Gretel, Cinderella, Little Red Riding Hood, and Snow White and the Seven Dwarfs living amidst the flowers. The figures, just child-height, were created and hand carved by the skilled artisans of the Black Forest in Germany.

Rivaling the floral beauty at Busch Gardens is the shimmering color of the hundreds of birds which comprise one of the largest avian displays in the world. On the spacious lawns of the Gardens and in the three large lagoons, the birds fly free and live in an environment much like their natural habitat. Pink flamingos, the brilliant natives of the African wilds, habitually flock together. The clusters of flamingos at Busch Gardens are like bright jewels set against a green background washed with Florida sunlight. In the lagoons, which are stocked with goldfish, hundreds of water birds make their homes. There are ducks of all varieties, geese, cranes and the long-legged ibis. Here, too, are the beautiful white swans, their graceful arched necks reflected in the water, black swans and the trumpeter swan, the rarest and perhaps most exquisite member of this elegant family.

Birds with a dazzling array of colored plumage capture the eye on

Ornamental grasses such as the giant reed and bambusa are planted throughout the Gardens for the bold effects they achieve.

In three covered and vine-enclosed arbors, arranged as resting areas, are many rare parrots in airy hanging cages.

Exotic animals such as the springbok, a graceful South African gazelle, and bright macaws take their place at Busch with exotic plants like the bird-of-paradise.

every side. Here one can see, but hardly believe, the toucans with their raven bodies and large multi-colored bills. There are friendly macaws in several varieties, cockatoos with sulphur or rose crests, and the peacocks that proudly spread their enormous tail feathers into a fan of incredible blue. In three covered and vine enclosed arbors, arranged as resting areas and shelters from the vagrant showers, are many rare members of the parrot family in airy hanging cages. These brightly colored birds have all been trained to mimic human speech.

Nearby is the enormous geodesic dome, ninety-nine feet in diameter, constructed of gold anodized aluminum. In this large "space frame" there are sixty-five species of the Gardens' more exotic birds. Here we find the beautiful reddish egret, storks, the secretary bird and many other rare species. A pool in the aviary is fed by a bubbling spring which flows into the flamingo lagoon. In one part of the garden, called Eagle Canyon, the Great Bald Eagle can be seen in a replica of his natural environment. Through a mesh-covered passageway in the man-made rock canyon thirty feet high, one can watch the royal eagle.

The lush tropical garden, replete with wide lawns, was originally fifteen acres of sandy slope in an industrial park.

Not surprisingly in a semi-tropical climate,
Busch Gardens has several species of palm,
including the everglade and date palms.

Throughout the day, at an amphitheater carved out of a hillside, visitors are invited to see frequent shows where trained cockatoos and macaws, chosen for their size and beautiful coloring, perform with almost human intelligence.

The magnificently colored macaws are the most popular birds at Busch Gardens. There are several different species here, all decked in different colored finery. The greenwing is a flaming red beauty with emerald wings. The military macaw is multi-colored in green, blue and red. Scarlet macaws, as might be expected, have scarlet body feathers, but their wings and tails are a striking array of blues, gold, red and white.

The terrace of the Old Swiss House, a restaurant patterned after an eighteenth-century Swiss chalet in Lucerne, Switzerland, has a panoramic view of the Wild Animal Kingdom, the most recent and most spectacular addition to Busch Gardens. It encompasses 186 acres of landscaped hills, mountains and rivers. It is built to duplicate, as nearly as possible, an African Veldt. Here on the "Congo River," "Lake Victoria," and "Mount Kilimanjaro," we find the rarest of wild animals flourishing in settings similar to their native homes.

Besides the more familiar giraffes, lions, white and black rhinos, Arabian camels, elephants, gorillas and chimpanzees, the Wild Animal Kingdom includes such lesser-known species as the tiny dik-dik, greater kudu, wildebeest, eland, gemsbok, Cape hartebeest, nyala, sitatunga, oryx, the Uganda kob, Lady Gray's waterbuck and the okapi, the rarest animal in captivity.

In the northwest section of the Kingdom is the forty-acre Survival Center where rare African animals are grouped into nucleus breeding herds. Endangered species are protected here, in a re-creation of their natural habitat, in the hope they will reproduce in sufficient quantities to restock other zoos and parks throughout the United States.

In the diversity of animal, bird and plant life and in the ingenious aspects of housing and display, Busch Gardens stands alone. It is by no means a conventional garden, but is, nonetheless, a place of great beauty dedicated to the incomparable variety of nature.

Along Storybook Lane, a dwarf village shaded by rhododendron in a forest setting features famous storybook characters.

Pink flamingos habitually flock together, but must share the lagoons with rare black swans and other waterfowl.

Theodore, Alabama

BELLINGRATH GARDENS

A Magnificent Garden Especially Celebrated for Its Azaleas

Courtesy Bellingrath Gardens

Iron lace work frames the patio of the
Bellingrath home, contrasting with colorful
seasonal flowers and old jumbo handmade bricks.

Opposite: Flamingos lend their exotic beauty
to the Oriental-American Garden at Bellingrath,
a sanctuary for two hundred species of birds.

In a lush tropical setting between Mobile, Alabama, and the Gulf of Mexico, there is a surprising sixty-acre garden where flowers bloom without interruption the year around. This is Bellingrath, the garden that got its start as a fishing camp. About fifty years ago Walter D. Bellingrath, who was destined to make a fortune from selling the then little-known drink Coca-Cola, brought his friends to hunt and fish here on the quiet banks of the Isle-aux-Oies River.

"Mr. Bell," as Bellingrath was affectionately known to the citizens of Mobile, was the industrious son of a German immigrant and a Scots-Irish Southern woman. He began his career at seventeen as a railroad station agent and telegraph operator for the Louisville and Nashville Railroad in the little Alabama town of Castleberry. In 1903 he moved to Mobile where, from a meager start at peddling the new "soda-pop" in a mule-drawn cart, he rose to a position of civic and business leadership in the community.

In 1917 Bellingrath bought the fishing camp on the Isle-aux-Oies River, and eight hundred acres of land owned in succession by American Indians, the French and the Spanish. It was here that the Spanish raised great Andalusian bulls for the bullrings of Spain. It was a site of great natural beauty with giant old oaks and pines on a wooded bluff overlooking the river stocked with fish. The rustic fishing lodge was fittingly called Bellecamp.

It was in these years that Mr. Bellingrath and his wife, the former Bessie Morse, became interested in gardening. In 1927 they traveled to Europe to see some of the famous gardens of the Old World, and brought back to Mobile a wealth of new ideas which they first tried in the gardens of their Mobile home. However, the idea of planting the acres at Bellecamp lurked alluringly in the back of their minds. Mrs. Bellingrath collected azaleas for the Mobile house. As the garden there filled to overflowing, the plants were moved out to the fishing camp on the river. The azaleas made such a brilliant display against the dark green of the woods and lush semi-tropical vegetation that it was no longer possible to resist the temptation to landscape the estate.

The Bellingrath home on the Isle-aux-Oies was designed in a Renaissance style by the well-known architect, George B. Rogers. Its hand-pressed antebellum bricks and traditional iron-lace grillwork give the aura of elegance, with overtones of old Spain and France, that typifies the architecture of the Southern Gulf Coast. A major feature of the house is the Bessie Morse Bellingrath collection of antiques, one of the best in the United States.

British landscape engineer A.A. Hunt was hired to develop the gardens. His qualifications ranged from four years of apprenticeship to eleven years of garden work in England, including work in the famous Royal Botanical Gardens at Kew. When completed, the Bellingrath estate was a masterpiece. Presided over by the mansion with its ever-changing floral display, the Gardens spread on one side down to the river, and on the other, to the emerald sparkle of the Great Lawn, past Mirror Lake to the Camellia Arboretum and the North Bayou.

In 1932 the Bellingraths issued an invitation to the people of Mobile to come see the beauty of azaleas in full bloom in their garden paradise. As word of its beauty spread, the response to the invitation was so overwhelming that the Bellingraths were forced to call the police to control the traffic between Mobile and their home. To reduce the throng of visitors to a manageable number, a small admission charge was initiated. This money, combined with substantial amounts of their own, was spent on improving the Gardens.

Mr. and Mrs. Bellingrath never seemed to mind the confusion created by their visitors. Even though he remained active in many business enterprises, Mr. Bell spent much of his time at the Gardens. He loved to wander or just to sit in his favorite lawn chair and talk to guests, especially children. He compared the garden to a lovely lady with fifty-two gowns, one for each week in the year. "There is no season here in the garden," he said. "We have beauty every day of the year."

And indeed the Bellingrath Gardens are beautiful the year around. The name Bellingrath has become a watchword for fine azaleas. Starting in the early spring (February in Alabama) to mid-April, a quarter of a million azaleas begin their blooming season. The best-loved species in the world: Indica, Kurume, Macrantha, Belgian and Rutherfordianas, all find their place in the spring spectrum, their colors varying from pink and salmon to deep rose, lavender, magenta, ivory, white and yellow.

Azaleas are found everywhere. Many are more than a hundred years old and range from fifteen to twenty feet high with a diameter of twenty to thirty feet. During the spring the vista from the house to the Great Lawn is literally ablaze with their glow of pink and white. In the Grotto beside the house, masses of azaleas hail the season, filling the huge stone urns along the flagstone steps and blossoming amid the shrubbery. At the boathouse on the river, where guests come by boat from nearby resorts, brilliant pink azaleas bloom before the first buds appear on the surrounding trees. On Mirror Lake at the center of the estate, white swans grace the dark waters, and azaleas create a panorama of color amid the branches of the old trees and vines. The beauty of the scene is doubled in the reflections on the lake.

Soon after the Mardi Gras in Mobile comes the city's annual Azalea Festival. Many of the area's private gardens are open to the public, and visitors come to see the thirty-five miles of Azalea Trail.

Throughout most of the Bellingrath estate, azaleas grow in a natural setting among the trees that originally grew at Bellecamp. There are more than seventy varieties of indigenous Southern trees,

Bromeliads, orchids and other exotic plants are on display in the Conservatory, where they grow summer and winter.

Opposite: Mr. Bellingrath compared his garden to a lovely lady with fifty-two gowns, one for each week in the year.

From the patio, the South Terrace with its surrounding trees illustrates why the Gardens are the "Charm Spot of the Deep South."

The Grotto at azalea time hails the season with masses of blooms filling the urns along the flagstone steps.

Courtesy Bellingrath Gardens

including magnolia, bay, cedar, holly, dogwood, hickory, beech, sourwood, cherry, pine and practically every variety of live oak. In addition to the evergreen azaleas, Bellingrath also has a fine collection of the native species (wood honeysuckle) in white, pink, yellow, cream and orange, which are naturalized in the woodlands.

As the spring progresses the azaleas are joined by masses of tulips, ranging from white to yellow, red and even black. Magnolias, dogwoods, hydrangeas, calla lilies, Easter lilies, Japanese and day lilies all follow in their season to create an endless chain of spectacular color.

In the area just south of the house is a lovely garden with fountains, tall oaks and hedges. A red granite monolith tells the story of the garden and another fountain with a bronze plaque tells the Biblical tale of Rebecca at the well. In the spring this formal area is alight with flowers. Around the Rebecca at the Well Pool, pink, white and purple amaryllis blend with tall, graceful white Easter lilies. Around the monolith, hydrangeas, aspidistra, nun orchids and *Mahonia japonica* make a colorful display in the late spring. The rockery nearby, a special project of Mrs. Bellingrath's, features spring wildflowers in their natural state.

Opposite: The Rose Garden, planted to resemble the emblem of the Rotary Club, is in bloom almost nine months of the year.

Presided over by the mansion, the gardens
spread on one side to the Great Lawn and North
Bayou, and on the other, down to the river.

On Mirror Lake at the center of the
estate, azaleas create a panorama of
color amid the branches of trees and vines.

Courtesy Bellingrath Gardens

Spring passes into summer and the silence of languid, hot days descends on Bellingrath. Bright sunlight drifts through the branches of the tall oak trees with their shrouds of Spanish moss shading the garden paths — paths silent except for the hum of bees and the splash of water.

In contrast to Northern summers which can scorch a garden with arid heat, the tropical showers of a Bellingrath summer bring more flowers to life in the verdant, semi-tropical climate. Masses of bright marigolds and beds of multicolored zinnias bloom.

Northern visitors are amazed at the sight of thousands of velvet-leafed African violets which bloom all summer in Bellingrath's rock garden. In the rose garden, day-flowering African water lilies, Nymphea hybrids, brighten the ponds with sparks of color. The formal gardens are alive now with yellow Delaware chrysanthemums and bright orange Dutch hybrid amaryllis.

With fall and Indian Summer come the second pride of Bellingrath Gardens, the camellias. *Camellia sasanqua* varieties begin blooming in early September and by November both *Camellia sasanqua* and *Camellia japonica* varieties, with colors ranging from pure white to a delicate shell pink and from rose pink to crimson, are in full bloom. In 1956 a special Camellia Arboretum was built in the western part of the garden so guests could enjoy the beauty of some nine hundred varieties of *Camellia japonica* and see their comparative merits under the same growing conditions. Some of the plants stand twelve to twenty feet tall, and with their colorful blooms they rival a beautifully decorated Christmas tree.

In the late fall the Great Lawn is bordered with a massive display of chrysanthemums and cassias in yellow, red and white.

By December, though the leaves have fallen from the great oak trees, the magic of color has not left the Gardens. The green of holly and evergreen plants is brighter than ever. Just before Christmas Bellingrath comes alive with the miracle of poinsettias whose top leaves, or bracts, turn at this time to the lively reds synonymous with the Christmas season.

And even in the Christmas season there is the promise of spring at Bellingrath. In December the many-colored crocuses push their way through the soil, to be followed in January and February by pansies, sweet alyssum, hyacinths, spirea, daffodils, anemones, dogwood and English daisies. The spring has begun again and the calendar of color here completes its circle without rest.

In some parts of the garden there are flowers almost the year around. In the Conservatory, orchids and other tropical plants grow summer and winter. The Rose Garden with twenty-five varieties of roses, laid out in the shape of a modified Rotary emblem, is in bloom nine months of the year. A bridge, made of jumbo handmade brick and iron-lace grillwork, is strategically situated to provide a view of both the Rose Garden and the Conservatory.

The latest of the new features that are constantly being added is an Oriental-American Garden on a pond south of Mirror Lake. It adjoins the rest of the garden, but is completely separated by its own unique architecture, tall trees and a combination of Oriental and American flowers. Here, where water cascades over a series of

This rustic wooden bridge is one of three at Bellingrath. The others are a high-arched Oriental bridge and a brick one with iron work.

Opposite: Flagstones with leaf designs pave one of the home's terraces where palms complement the lushness of tropical growth.

Below: Balcony, grillwork and flowering patio clearly show the mingling of Mediterranean and French influences in the Bellingrath home.

Winston Pote from A. Devaney, N.Y.

flat rocks, bright pink flamingos accent the arch of an Oriental bridge and a replica of a Japanese teahouse.

Bellingrath is a haven for hundreds of varieties of birds and animals. The growing deer herd is carefully protected. At least two hundred species of birds either stay here the year around or stop off during their migration. The story goes that a number of tame peacocks once proudly displayed their finery about the garden; but, to the terror of some of the lady visitors, the birds showed a rather voracious taste for costume jewelry, and had to be banished.

A less troublesome group of birds makes its home in the Bellingrath visitors' lounge. In 1967, O.H. Delchamps, Alfred Delchamps and their sister Mrs. Wayne S. Moore, of a well-known Mobile philanthropic family, donated their peerless collection of Boehm porcelain to Bellingrath Gardens. Boehm, an artist from Trenton, New Jersey, is world famous for his birds and other porcelain figurines in life-like colors. His works, fired by methods used over two thousand years ago in China, are displayed at the White House, the Metropolitan Museum of Art, Buckingham Palace, the Vatican and the Royal Palace in Stockholm, as well as in many private collections. The Delchamps collection, however, is the largest in the world. The eighty-six pieces, varying in size from a few inches to the magnificent seven-foot ivory-billed woodpecker, are displayed in the visitors' lounge in glass cases which can be viewed from both the outside and the inside of the building. A single pair of song sparrows in the collection is valued at $50,000.

Over the Gardens' beauty, the spirit of Mr. and Mrs. Bellingrath remains a living presence. To show its appreciation, Mobile honored "Mr. Bell" for his "unexcelled contributions to the economic, civic, cultural and religious life of the community" and expressed "specific eternal gratefulness to him for his creation of the gardens." After Mrs. Bellingrath's death in 1943, Mr. Bellingrath continued to build upon her dream of a beautiful garden for all to see. In 1950 he gave the estate in trust to the Bellingrath-Morse Foundation. In the deed to the foundation on February 1, 1950, Mr. Bellingrath carried out one further wish that the childless couple always cherished, that the proceeds of the garden be "devoted to the intellectual and religious upbuilding of young men and women of our Southland, as well as to foster and perpetuate those Christian values which were recognized by our forefathers as essential for the building of a great nation."

The proceeds of the garden now go to several Southern colleges: Southwestern at Memphis, Huntington College at Montgomery and Stillman College at Tuscaloosa, along with Mobile's Central Presbyterian and the St. Francis Street Methodist churches.

Mr. Bellingrath died on August 8, 1955, just two days after his eighty-sixth birthday. The Bellingrath house, with its collection of priceless antiques, was opened to the public in 1956. This lovely home and magnificent garden on the Isle-aux-Oies River are willed to the public, the Bellingraths' only heirs.

Lookout Mountain, Tennessee

ROCK CITY GARDENS

A Geologic Treasure Enhanced by Woodland Flora

High atop Lookout Mountain in the Chattanooga area of Tennessee is a place that seems at first to be less a garden and more a natural phenomenon. This is Rock City Gardens, which lies among spectacular rock formations created by millions of years of erosion and upheaval in the mountains of Appalachia.

The place may have taken its name in 1823 from two visiting missionaries who observed that it looked like a tall city all of rock. Channels, which looked like streets, were cut through the rock by rushing water. Indeed, the rock formations, like thousand-ton Balanced Rock, the Needle's Eye, and the Cave of the Winds, and the view from Rock City over miles of rolling, sun-swept countryside, are so overwhelming that visitors often overlook the beautiful plant specimens to be found here.

The Civil War battle for Lookout Mountain, which stretches half a mile above sea level, was christened by imaginative newspapermen as "The Battle above the Clouds" because it was fought above the clouds which often swirl around the mountain's peak.

In 1924 ten acres of this sculptured land was bought by Mr. and Mrs. Garnet Carter. Freida Carter, a talented artist and musician, directed workmen in laying paths through the city of rock that wound around the cliffside. She set out to replant the "garden" with every species of tree, flower and shrub native to the area. When she was finished, the Garden Club of America awarded her its Bronze Medal of Distinction for outstanding achievement in horticulture and conservation.

Noting the growing beauty of his wife's work, Mr. Carter, whose invention of miniature golf and "Tom Thumb" golf courses had become an international craze, put his inventive mind to work on a large-scale promotional campaign for Rock City. The Gardens, opened to the public in 1933, were an instant success. The hundreds of visitors quickly swelled to thousands. As the money from admissions came in, the Carters put it right back into the Gardens. Paths were smoothed to flagstone walks. Better bridges and protective walls were built. New views were created as new sections of the trail were opened.

The wonders of nature, in all of its aspects, are found in Rock City. Paths wind through and around giant boulders and down into deep caverns. A 180-foot swinging bridge stretches above the Cave of the Winds where the mountain breezes evoke the sound of a

The Gardens have over four hundred different species of plants native to the Lookout Mountain region.

Opposite: Rock City would not have evolved without the incessant action of water. The work still goes slowly forward.

rushing sea. Rainbow Hall is a passageway of stone, including panes of colored glass, overlooking the vista of the Great Smokies.

Visitors are often surprised to find the imprint of sea shells on the rock high on the mountainside here. Yet 240 million years ago, a vast ocean covered most of the interior of the North American continent. The Appalachian Mountains evolved forty million years later (200 million years ago) when a tremendous upheaval tossed the ocean bottom thousands of feet upward. The mountains thus created were higher than the Rocky Mountains are today, or the Alps in Europe. Then, twenty million years ago, the area around Lookout Mountain was ground down by erosion. And once again it was heaved upward to produce new mountains, now known as the Cumberlands. Lookout Mountain is part of the Cumberland chain. As a result of these two eras of great upheaval and erosion, Lookout Mountain was left with a fascinating conglomeration of rock including the fossil-bearing limestone, and a hard sandstone cap out of which the strange rock formations are carved.

At Lover's Leap where, as this legend always goes, an Indian maiden jumped to her death after the tribal execution of her lover, a ninety-foot waterfall hurtles down the mountainside to a pool below. The many streams and waterfalls on Lookout Mountain continue the work of erosion started millions of years ago. Mushroom Rock, in the shape of a giant mushroom, shows the capriciousness of nature, while a narrow cleft, called Fat Man's Squeeze, puts even thin people into close contact with the sheer rock walls.

Throughout these rock formations is Mrs. Carter's "garden": the awesome sight of a lone pine tree, clinging to a pinnacle of wind-swept rock; a clump of honeysuckle heavily laden with fragrant, opened flowers. Of the more than four hundred different kinds of plants at Rock City, all are grown exactly as they would be in their natural state. There are no labels (though guides will answer questions about plant life), only miles of woodland flora to signal the changing of the seasons.

In whatever season, Rock City reveals a majestic natural beauty. In spring, around the streams and water holes, delicate maidenhair ferns *(Adiantum pedatum)* and sword ferns *(Nephrolepis biserrata)* are only two of the types that mingle with early violets and unfolding "wake robins" or trilliums. Through the shaded hollows of the mountainside the pink and white blossoms of wild honey-suckle *(Azalea nudiflora)*, mountain rose bay *(Rhododendron catawbiense)*, great laurel *(R. maximum)*, mountain laurel *(Kalmia latifolia)*, peach *(Prunus persica)* and wild cherry *(Prunus avium)* add bright touches to the green of the newly awakening forest.

Many of the flowers, such as wild azaleas and hydrangeas, gentians and the friendly winking black-eyed Susans, are familiar to garden visitors. Others are less widely known. Galax *(Galax*

Nearly half a mile above sea level, a
patch of daffodils overlooks the valley.

Right: With the help of wind and ice, slightly acid rain-streams have scooped out amazing rock formations.

Opposite: The difference in hardness between sandstone and limestone accounts for rock formations sculpted by wind and water.

Below: Looking out from this grotto, visitors see a blending of the natural and the man-made typical of Rock City.

Below: Lover's Leap Falls, almost ninety feet high, makes a most peculiar rumbling noise when heard at a distance.

Above: Seen through a handmade arch, the 180-foot-long swinging bridge spans deep chasms and dizzying heights.

aphylla), with lovely heart-shaped evergreen leaves once grew abundantly on Lookout Mountain. Since it has become popular with florists as a substitute for ivy, it is almost extinct in its wild form. The tiny rattlesnake-weed *(Hieracium venosum),* with its low-growing white flower, has long been used by mountain folk as a cure for snake bite. New Jersey tea *(Ceanothus americanus),* a low-growing shrub was commonly used by Indians and also by early pioneers as a substitute for British tea.

Through the summer, blossoms and berries fill the woodlands at Rock City. The brilliant red-orange of the trumpet creeper, the flowers of the spiny prickly pear, the bloom of orange milkweed and delicate passion flowers can be seen along the paths. Huckleberries, elderberries, blackberries and the mountain favorite, black haw, grow wild in the woods. Visitors are requested not to pick the fruits or flowers.

Hot August days and the beginning of fall, so often a dreary time in the garden, is one of the most beautiful seasons at Rock City. As summer draws to a close, a blue haze hangs over the mountain. The sweet scent of goldenrod, whose crushed leaves have the odor of licorice, blankets the hillsides, as does its less abundant brother, the silver-rod, the single white species of goldenrod. Thistle flowers bloom and seed, and the purple ironweed grows on tall stalks.

The trees, a background for the flowers of spring and summer, now make a show of their own. Rock City comes alive with the color of red and gold-leafed maples, red oak and white oak, Southern red cedar, and the dark leaves of the American elm, the sycamore, the light golden foliage of birch and the leaves of dozens of other beautiful native species. The evergreen trees — hemlock, spruce and pine, as well as the evergreen leaves of mountain laurel and other shrubs — make a vivid green backdrop for the brilliant colors of the deciduous foliage.

Even as winter descends on the slopes of Lookout Mountain, the green of moss, teaberry, partridge berry and evergreen shrubs, the brown of lichen and the pinnacles of jagged rock make Rock City a stately and beautiful garden.

The garden acres are off limits to hunters, and one often sees the deer, squirrels, and chipmunks that take shelter there. The golden sweep of hummingbirds is a common sight. Orioles, vireos, woodpeckers, robins, blue jays and dozens of others nest in the forest.

Complementing the natural beauty of the garden is the work of the human laborers. The fine stonework of Gnomes Overpass is a typical tribute to the work of mountain craftsmen.

Although Garnet and Freida Carter were childless, they had a particular regard for the interests of children who visited Rock City. They soon discovered that whatever was designed to attract children had equal fascination for adults. Goblin's Underpass, the Hall of the Mountain King and Rainbow Hall were built. Little gnome figurines were made and placed along the trail.

In 1947 one of Rock City's greatest attractions was completed. This is Fairyland Caverns, a collection of almost life-size ceramic figurines in underground fairyland settings. Cinderella, Hansel and Gretel, Rip Van Winkle, Snow White and a recently added Mother Goose Village are happily at home in this favorite setting. The entrance to the grottoes is guarded by a crystal underground falls. Fluorescent colors and magical black light are used to accent the fairyland figures.

The facilities of Rock City are continually being improved. Places where guests frequently step off the path to "get a better view" or to take photographs, are usually incorporated into the path itself, and the necessary guard rails put up. Yet, for all the man-made attractions, the greatest appeal of Rock City is the natural majesty so dramatically revealed in the giant rocks and woodlands. This has been so since the Indians first saw this wondrous land, and it always will be.

Garden officials state that it takes good vision and a cloudless day to prove their claim that seven states are visible from Lookout Mountain.

Unlike plants in gardens designed for floral display, Rock City's plants grow in their natural environment.

Georgetown, Washington, D. C.
DUMBARTON OAKS
Elegant Garden on an Historic Estate

This fountain and staircase below the Green Garden is decorated with reliefs of bulrushes and sculptured foliage.

Opposite: The Urn Terrace at Dumbarton Oaks takes its name from a charming sculptured stone urn atop a tall, fluted pedestal.

The story of the garden at Dumbarton Oaks in Washington, D.C.'s old Georgetown section, is essentially the story of a friendship between two famous American women — Mrs. Robert Woods Bliss, wife of the former United States diplomat and Ambassador to Argentina, and Mrs. Beatrix Farrand, a world-renowned landscape architect.

Through years of travel in Europe with her husband, Mrs. Bliss cherished the dream of a garden of her own as lovely as those she saw in France and England and Italy. In 1920, returned from assignment at the U.S. Embassy in Paris, Mr. and Mrs. Bliss purchased the huge old estate at 32nd and R Streets in Washington, Dumbarton Oaks. Although the estate was overgrown and run-down, it had some magnificent large trees and a fine view of the wooded Rock Creek ravine. It was here that Mrs. Bliss' dream of a great garden was to come true.

The land was originally deeded to a Scotsman named Ninian Beall, in about 1702. He called it The Rock of Dumbarton, after a landmark in Dumbarton on the Clyde, the town where he was born. The property remained in the Beall family for nearly eighty years. In 1823 it was purchased by James Edward Calhoun, whose more famous brother, John C. Calhoun, often stayed there while he served as vice-president under John Quincy Adams. The house changed names and owners several more times before 1920 when Mr. and Mrs. Bliss bought the handsome Georgian mansion with its large park and many outbuildings.

Mr. Bliss was appointed Minister to Sweden in 1923 and in 1927 as Ambassador to Argentina, and Mrs. Bliss was looking for someone to design her garden while she was abroad. She wanted someone who would share her idea that a garden, as well as a house, should be a comfortable place for entertaining and everyday living. The person she found was Beatrix Farrand, and thus began a friendship which would last for forty years.

Beatrix Farrand was one of the youngest women ever elected to the American Society of Landscape Architects. Her training in Europe and her study with Professor Charles Sprague Sargent at Boston's Arnold Arboretum gave her a vast knowledge of gardening. She was the consulting landscape architect for Princeton University, and later the University of Chicago and Yale University. Her private practice included gardens for J. Pierpont Morgan, Mrs. John D. Rockefeller, Jr., Mrs. Theodore Roosevelt and Mrs. Woodrow Wilson. But for all these fine commissions, Mrs. Farrand believed

A girl and deer stand watchfully near the Camellia Circle, a miniature garden outstanding in its own right.

that the work at Dumbarton Oaks was the best of her fifty years practice. To visit this garden is to realize that she was, indeed, a genius of landscape design.

The garden at Dumbarton Oaks was a considerable challenge from the point of view of gardening as well as landscaping. To the north of the big brick mansion, the land fell steeply down toward Rock Creek. Here the farm buildings stood, and a maze of dusty cow paths scarred the earth. Today this is the site of beautiful formal gardens and there is no evidence of its humble past.

Before the first spade of earth was turned, Mrs. Farrand submitted dozens of sketches for the owner's approval. This procedure was followed all through the design of the garden. There was frequent correspondence between Washington and wherever the Blisses happened to be stationed at the time. When Ambassador and Mrs. Bliss visited Washington, mock-ups of proposed designs were made and planting areas staked out for viewing on the scene. Nothing was done without the careful consideration of everyone concerned.

The first project, and one of the most difficult to construct, was the terracing to the east of the mansion. As with all good design, the plan seems to have been accomplished with ease, and today these terraces display great splendor and liveliness.

The Beech Terrace, shaded by a tall American beech tree, is a small informal setting with a canopy-covered seat in the eighteenth-century French style. In spring the ground is spangled with the flowers of scillas, snowdrops and other early bulbs. Because of its architecture, the garden is interesting in every season, but spring in Washington is a particularly beguiling time of year.

The nearby Green Garden, larger and more formal, was designed for large gatherings. Located behind the brick wall of the Orangery which is attached to the mansion, the Green Garden has fine marble tables and marble seats, potted lemon trees and garlanded trophies designed by Frederick Coles, a British stone carver. The only colors to challenge the green of lawn, ivy and tall oaks is the purple of wisteria growing against the Orangery wall and a few white azaleas and white wood hyacinths. Also considered in the design was the addition of the brightly colored dresses that the guests would wear. From the parapet here, one can see across Washington to the minaret of the Mohammedan mosque of Massachusetts Avenue, and in the foreground, down the gently graded stone steps to the swimming pool and Pebble Garden. Although the dresses of the visitors today may not have the elegance of those worn by the guests for whom the Green Garden was designed, the effect of swirling color is just as delightful.

Each garden ornament was chosen and placed with exquisite care. Some ornaments, such as the marble Provençal fountain in the Ellipse and the terra-cotta urn which originally formed the center of the Urn Terrace, were discovered by Mrs. Bliss in her travels and transported to Washington. Others such as the swimming pool fountain and the fountain in the Fountain Terrace were created

Right: Mrs. Bliss and Mrs. Farrand styled this fountain after an Italian street fountain. The niche and wall are covered with *rocaille*.

Below: Paired American hornbeams cut as an aerial-hedge form the setting for the Provençal fountain in the Ellipse.

Formerly an herb garden, the Arbor Terrace is entirely paved and its two levels are divided by baroque scrolls of Doria stone from Italy.

Opposite: The statues of smiling boys holding dolphins in the pools of the Fountain Terrace might have come from an old French garden.

especially for Dumbarton Oaks. Models of all of these were first prepared for Mrs. Bliss to view and approve.

The sound of splashing water fills the terraces below the Green Garden. In the middle of the steps leading down to the swimming pool, a stone basin catches water as it drips from a sculptured shell. The swimming pool itself, a picture of quiet European elegance, is bordered by delicate pollarded weeping willows, wisteria, azaleas and cherry trees. The nearby Pebble Garden, a tremendous mosaic of small stones laid by Vincent de Benedetto, is shallowly covered with water from a central fountain of lead figures. This can be viewed from an upper walkway and, indeed, it is only from high above that the grandeur of its conception can be fully appreciated.

From here, the gardens become less formal as they recede from the house. A brick path leads to Crab Apple Hill with its wide expanse of lawn and displays of narcissus in the spring, and iris and peonies in the early summer. Beyond, on Forsythia Hill, hundreds of naturalized forsythia which surround the trunks of silver maple and tulip trees, challenge the golden brightness of the sun. On Cherry Hill several varieties of cherry trees join the more famous cherry blossoms of Washington in their spring splendor. Here the garden seems to merge into the park behind it. This was, in fact, once part of the Dumbarton Oaks estate. With its spring house, mill and fish ponds, it was donated in 1940 by Mr. and Mrs. Bliss to the Department of the Interior's National Park Service. These three informal areas surround the more formal Ellipse, where paired

Courtesy Dumbarton Oaks

Above: Beneath high-arching silver maples, Mélisande's Allée displays drifts of lilies of the valley and stars-of-Bethlehem.

Right: The gardens contain an apparently endless series of intimate nooks, room-like spaces and covered walks.

American hornbeams, cut as an aerial-hedge, form the setting for the Provençal fountain.

To the east of Cherry Hill, paths lead to a series of secluded garden areas that many consider to be the most delightful in the whole of Dumbarton Oaks. The tiny Camellia Circle, almost hidden by dense foliage, boasts beautiful camellias in season. From time to time during the spring and summer, primulas, lilies of the valley, and rose and white wood-hyacinths flower brightly beneath a sculptured Italian urn full of flowers. Mélisande's Allée is a meadow of flowers that might have come straight from Maeterlinck's tale of Pelléas and Mélisande. Scattered here on the grass under silver maples, are blue scillas, stars-of-Bethlehem and more lilies of the valley. Up a short flight of steps, past a rustic stone seat, another meadow blooms in April with yellow daffodils and white narcissus.

From here the path leads to the restful seclusion of Lover's Lane Pool and its amphitheater backed with stone columns and urns. With these three gardens Mrs. Farrand achieved a quality of timelessness that makes if difficult to believe that they have been here only since the 1920's.

Near Lover's Lane Pool a stone walk and steps that pass beneath a huge copper beech tree lead back to the formal gardens. The Fountain Terrace is a delightful French garden whose borders are changed with the seasons. First tulips, then sweet William, borage, columbine, coral bells and foxglove and, in the fall, a spectacular

Above: Even the seemingly natural parts of the gardens are as much works of art as the famous formal terraces.

Below: The Box Walk is lined with the only surviving box plantings originally conceived by the Blisses.

Courtesy Dumbarton Oaks

Courtesy Dumbarton Oaks

The most evocative place in the gardens is Lover's Lane Pool and Amphitheater, which might have been transported to Washington from an old Italian garden.

show of bright crysanthemums here surrounds two lovely fountains. Nearer the house, the formal English Rose Garden takes its design from the gardens so popular in England in the seventeenth and eighteenth centuries. Specimen English and American boxwood bushes contrast sharply with the red, yellow and white of roses. Finally, in this area is the Urn Terrace with a carved stone replica of a fine terra-cotta urn purchased in France by Mrs. Bliss.

In addition to a seemingly endless series of other intimate nooks and room-like spaces which we leave for the visitor himself to discover, another major garden area remains. The great North Vista, leading from the mansion for almost the full length of the garden, is bordered with stone walls and pillars and appears from the house to be an immense stretch of lawn. From the bottom of the terrace the optical illusion is revealed as the terraces, the last as long as the preceding two, rise in a series of connecting steps back to the house. This technique, so successfully used by Mrs. Farrand, was first employed by Italian artists such as Bernini and Barromini. Beatrix Farrand, unfortunately, did not live to see the North Vista completed. It was finished by her associate, Miss Ruth Havey, with the assistance of Frederick Coles and Mrs. Bliss.

In the Green Garden, set into the north parapet overlooking the entire garden, Mr. and Mrs. Bliss placed a plaque in memory of the gardens' designer. It bears the following inscription:

DUMBARTON OAKS
SOMNIA SUB PATULIS VIDEANT NASCENTIA RAMIS
SIDERA FAUSTA FERANT OMNIA ET USQUE BONA

TESTIMONIO AMICITIAE
BEATRICIS FARRAND

NEC ILLORUM IMMEMORES QUI POSTERO AEVO
VITAS VERITATI ERVENDAE IMPENDERINT
HANC TABELLAM POSUERUNT
ROBERTUS WOODS BLISS UXORQUE MILDRED

"May they see dreams springing from the spreading boughs, may fortunate stars always bring them good omens.

"Dedicated to the friendship of Beatrix Farrand and mindful of those who in a later age shall spend their lives bringing forth the truth.

"This tablet has been placed by Robert Woods Bliss and his wife Mildred."

In 1940 Ambassador and Mrs. Bliss donated their garden as well as the mansion and its collection of art and its library to Harvard University as a center for Byzantine studies. A magnificent small museum designed by the renowned architect Philip Johnson, was opened in 1963 for the display of Mr. Bliss' unparalleled collection of pre-Columbian art. A garden library containing Mrs. Bliss' collection of books on landscape architecture has also been opened to those with a special interest in the field.

The fine old estate, which in 1944 saw the famous four-power conference to draw up proposals for the United Nations, is now a place for work and study. The gardens, which maintain their original elegance, are a continuing source of joy and inspiration to an appreciative public.

Above: This column and vase is a replica of the "terrior's" tomb in Naples, where a terrier dog was buried by an Italian lady who was unable to pronounce properly her pet's name.

Right: The Pebble Garden, a mosaic of small stones laid by Vincent de Benedetto, contains a fountain with lead figures.

WINTERTHUR

Henry F. du Pont's Masterpiece

"A beautiful garden I think of as being a work of art," Henry F. du Pont once said, "but unlike a painting or book, a garden grows and always changes."

Mr. du Pont, who was one of America's most famous gardeners, loved flowers all his life. As a schoolboy at boarding school, this young scion of the du Pont family chose to spend his spare time with a local nurseryman.

He was born at Winterthur, the son of Colonel Henry Algernon du Pont, a Civil War hero and senator from Delaware. Even as a young man Henry du Pont began to formulate his gardening ideas. He was particularly intrigued by the profusion of spring flowers growing around his father's house: snowdrops, crocuses, squills, daffodils, irises, and other small bulbs and perennials. As early as 1900 he began the work of increasing their number in a naturalized planting. By 1910 the area known as March Walk was established and now — still one of the loveliest areas at Winterthur — it extends from the house to the large old saucer magnolia at the bend of the back drive. After the snow melts from the winter-bound earth of the garden, brilliant yellow *Adonis amurensis* show their heads along with thousands of delicate mauve *Crocus tomasinianus*. This is the fascinating season of the squills, snowdrops, the species iris, daffodils and other glowing harbingers of spring. The March Walk continues to be of interest beyond the spring. The early bulbs are followed by violets, anemones, bellworts, Virginia bluebells and others that bloom until late summer.

Around 1914 Henry du Pont and his father began planting the Winterthur Pinetum, now one of the largest collections of both rare and native conifers in the Eastern United States. The rich fragrance and green color of the pines makes this a favored place the year around. In the winter the boughs are frosted with snow, and in spring the trees form a solid green backdrop for the beauty of the flowers that abound on all sides. Here we find the sharp-needled, tiger-tail spruce, the dragon spruce and one of the finest specimens of the fabled dawn redwood in the country, as well as examples of most other well-known evergreens.

The Winterthur estate dates back to 1839. James Bidermann, son-in-law of E.I. du Pont, who founded the du Pont Company, then bought some 450 acres of land in Christiana Hundred, New Castle County, near the du Pont powder mill on the banks of the Brandywine Creek. Two years later Bidermann traveled to Europe

The gardens are noted for their azaleas, which emblazon their delicate hues of pink and red on the wide expanses of green.

Opposite: The original formal pattern of the gardens at Winterthur has given way to Henry du Pont's concept of naturalized plantings.

Directional barriers along the tanbark
walks and turf paths are changed almost daily
to guide visitors to the best vistas.

with his wife, the former Evelina du Pont, and hired a French architect to design the estate which he called Winterthur after the city in Switzerland where his family had lived.

The grounds at Winterthur were laid out in a formal plan with a small sunken garden, which as early as 1859 was acclaimed as a local beauty spot. In 1867 Bidermann's son sold Winterthur to his mother's brother, Henry du Pont, and the estate has been in the family ever since.

The original formal pattern of the gardens has given way to Henry F. du Pont's concept of naturalized plantings. His idea was to create informal masses of color to be seen against the indigenous trees and rolling Delaware hills.

The gardens today show the hand of a master craftsman. Along tanbark and turf paths, azaleas in delicate hues of pink and red emblazon their color against a dark green background. The design is as carefully considered as that of a great painting. In the Azalea Woods, under a tall canopy of tulip trees, flowering dogwood reveals its beautiful white bloom. These are arranged as an arch over huge beds of Kurume azaleas in a whole range of colors. Under these is a carpet of trilliums, green ferns, anemones, violets and blue and mauve scillas.

Every tree and plant grown in Delaware is represented at Winterthur, and native plants are seldom replaced by others. The exotics, instead, are grown side by side with native sprigs, and equal attention is given to each. Native American plants such as the brilliant scarlet cardinal flower and the yellow Indian-cup, varieties of rose and laurel, are carefully tended and propagated. Even the plants regarded as weeds are seldom eradicated. Existing trees are also treasured. According to the gardeners here, "A fully matured tree cannot be purchased at any price."

The museum at Winterthur, with one of the largest collections of American decorative arts to be found in this country, is a treasure-trove that should not be missed. Furnishing his home with early interior woodwork, furniture and other household objects was another of Henry du Pont's great interests. In 1951, when he moved from his family home to a smaller house, The Henry Francis du Pont Winterthur Museum was opened to the public (by appointment). Here are such rare period interiors as the one from a house built at Oyster Bay, Long Island, in the 1650's; the Hart Room, colonial Massachusetts around 1640; and the Port Royal Parlor, Philadelphia, 1762. Henry du Pont's formidable reputation as a connoisseur of art and antiques gained for him the confidence of Mrs. Jacqueline Kennedy who asked him to advise her on the selection of antiques when she was refurnishing the White House.

But the most famous aspect of the Winterthur estate is still its gardens which have steadily grown in beauty since their conception in the early 1900's. Flowing through a valley at the center of the property, Clenny Run makes its way to the Brandywine. The brook provides water for the gardens' several ponds as well as a lovely

Right: In May the Azalea Woods reach their height, displaying huge shrubs carefully selected for their colors.

Below: Though seemingly unplanned, the informal mass plantings were laid out according to creative designs and color arrangements.

setting for ferns and wildflowers and a natural watering place for wildlife.

Overlooking Clenny Run is Oak Hill, named for the large stand of oak trees planted there. It is one of the most beautiful features of the gardens. In the early 1900's, Delaware was struck by the chestnut blight which eventually destroyed all native American chestnut trees. The chestnuts at Winterthur were not spared, and by the 1920's, when the dead trees were removed, there were large bare patches in the once beautiful woods. Mr. du Pont decided to use these open spaces as a nursery for the first Kurume azaleas to grow in this country. They did so well here that their beauty soon equaled that of the beech, oak and tulip-trees. The "nursery" had itself become part of the gardens.

In the 1950's, with a display of late color in mind, the Oak Hill area was planted with Glenn Dale azaleas, spirea, mock orange and deutzia. On a neighboring hill the Bristol Summerhouse was built to take advantage of the excellent view of Clenny Run and the surrounding valley.

Kurumes were the first azaleas grown at Winterthur. Mr. du Pont saw them in 1917 at the Japanese exhibit at the San Francisco Exposition. They had never before been shown in this country and he acquired seventeen of the new plants. The Winterthur gardeners soon set about propagating them. Even today the beautiful, many-hued Kurume azaleas are among the most important flowers to be seen here. In addition to the plantings in the Azalea Woods, hundreds of them blend their brilliance with the rich green foliage in other areas of the gardens.

Because of the tremendous number of azaleas at Winterthur, great care is taken to achieve the right blend of color without over-powering the eye or making the planting seem artificial. Drifts of the beautiful flowers are blended so subtly that it is impossible for the untrained eye to see where one shade ends and another begins.

White azaleas, sometimes grown alone, and countless wildflowers are used to soften the effect of their other, brighter neighbors. Among the native American wildflowers are blue, yellow and white violets, rue-anemone, Jacob's ladder, blue phlox, trillium, jack-in-the-pulpit and Virginia bluebells. Wildflowers from other countries include the English primroses, European periwinkle, and blue Eurasian squills and chionodoxas. Several varieties of fern lend their delicate greens to the woodland floor. The total effect — bright azaleas, dark trees, flashes of wildflower color — is one of indescribable beauty.

Only two gardens remain at Winterthur that might be considered formal. Peonies, which do not lend themselves to naturalized planting, are set most beautifully in one of the formal areas. These plantings extend down a terraced path, and a latticed summerhouse completes the picture. Throughout most of the United States the peony is thought of as the big, double Chinese species *Peonia albiflora sinensis* that blooms at the end of May. None of those at

Opposite: A brook flows through a valley at the center of the property, providing water for the gardens' several ponds.

Above: Trees are treasured, as evidenced by the Winterthur gardeners who say, "A fully matured tree cannot be purchased at any price."

Below: Because of the large number of azaleas, great care is taken to achieve the right blend of color without overpowering the eye.

The Pinetum, begun around 1914, now has one of the largest collections of both rare and native conifers in the Eastern United States.

Below: In spring the trees form a solid backdrop for the beauty of the flowers that abound on all sides.

Winterthur is of the conventional type. They are all magnificent Japanese, French and Chinese hybrids of both the tree and herbaceous type. All of the hybrids were created by A.P. Saunders, a world-famous hybridist from Clinton, New York. One of the eight peony beds alone contains forty-one varieties of this beautiful flower. Unlike the usual peonies, those at Winterthur bloom from the first week in May, starting with the yellow Daystar and continuing throughout the season. The colors of the Saunders hybrids vary from red to ivory, yellow, pink and white, with lush green foliage unrivaled by traditional peonies.

The other formal area is the Sundial Garden. Here, around an armillary sundial, grow formal beds of dwarf evergreen privet-honeysuckle, white spirea, pink flowering almond, and pink and salmon flowering quince. This garden is best seen in late April. The blossoming trees and shrubs, including lilacs, cherry, magnolia and Chinese snowball form a delicate pink and white contrast to the soft blue of phlox and the dark green background of the Pinetum.

Though Winterthur has a staff of more than fifty working in the gardens, a fire department, and a tree surgeon who works every day, Henry du Pont considered himself the head gardener until his death in 1969. He was regularly up and working in his room by 6:30 a.m. At 9 o'clock he set off on a morning tour of the gardens. He was never without a notebook in which he set down an endless list of gardening projects and ideas.

Two of the latest to be completed are a mile-long walk through Chandler Woods, a forest bordering the estate, and a "textured garden" of shrubs and plants on the wall of an old rock quarry.

The Quarry, located below the Bristol Summerhouse, is a quiet world in itself. The huge rocks jutting out from the sides of the cliff provide a cool, moist place for myriads of small wildflowers even on

There is a staff of more than fifty working in the gardens, a fire department and a tree surgeon who is in daily attendance.

Every tree and plant grown in Delaware is represented at Winterthur, and these native plants are the dominant feature.

Left: One of the latest projects to be
completed is a mile-long walk through a quiet
forest on the border of the estate.

Below: The total effect of the woodlands—
bright azaleas, dark trees, flashes of
wildflower color—is one of great beauty.

the warmest of summer days. The base of the Quarry is spring fed. Above the Quarry grow dwarf forsythia, dwarf bearded iris, satsuki azaleas and cyclamen. In its boggy base are marvelous primulas of many kinds. In early spring there is *Primula denticulata*, a hardy native of the Himalayas with mauve or white blossoms the size and shape of tennis balls. In late spring and early summer, tall candelabra primulas of all colors appear throughout the Quarry where tall oaks and beeches grow, and give shade to a secluded terrace on one side.

As the streams flow from the Quarry they are dammed into ponds, many of them stocked with fish. Water is important here for reservoirs in the dry season, for accents of coolness in the gardens, and as a watering place for animals, both wild and tame, that live on the estate. Flowers sparkle on the edges of ponds, and on many of the arched stone bridges that span the stream, roses grow.

Birds of all kinds stay at Winterthur. The heron poses, a silent, one-legged sentinel. In the ponds, ducks and Canada geese swim noisily. Special islands in the reservoir harbor the native waterfowl. The many birds common to Delaware — robins, sparrows, chickadees, nuthatches, crows, cardinals and tiny goldfinches — bathe in the springs and build their nests here. Other birds stop off on their way each year to a warmer climate. Every autumn a solitary loon stops here to ring the woods with his wild, piercing call. It is not uncommon to catch a glimpse of a fleeting deer or to spot a raccoon or groundhog. Squirrels are regular residents as are one or two inconspicuous foxes.

In 1951 Mr. du Pont deeded his home to an educational and charitable foundation he had established in 1930, to be opened to the public as the Winterthur Museum. In 1962 he became the first American vice-president of the Royal Horticultural Society of England. Until his death, at 88, a young-hearted Henry du Pont worked at the challenging task of maintaining Winterthur as one of the most beautiful gardens in the nation.

Above right: The 450 acres which now make up Winterthur were originally bought by James Bidermann, son-in-law of E.I. du Pont.

Bottom right: In addition to its floral attractions, the gardens contain ducks and Canada geese which swim noisily in the ponds.

Towson, Maryland

HAMPTON NATIONAL HISTORIC SITE

An Authentic Segment of Early Maryland

A stone urn on the grounds of the historic site enhances the authenticity of this segment of early Maryland.

Opposite: The formal garden and the house at Hampton National Historic Site date from the years immediately following the Revolution.

In May 1949, when Hampton was opened to the public by the Society for the Preservation of Maryland Antiquities, Governor William P. Lane addressed the assembled crowd. "I am profoundly grateful," he said, "to note the great increase in popular interest in the preservation of our incomparable heritage.... The ever increasing crowds of visitors to our historic shrines and growth of local and national organizations devoted to this work are sources of much reassurance that we shall not waste our historic substance, that we shall revere, treasure and defend all that made us what we are."

Public interest in the preservation of parks, woodlands and historic landmarks continues to intensify in this country. Hampton National Historic Site is but one of many great estates retained for the pleasure and benefit of the public at large. The rambling old Maryland home with forty acres of woods and gardens was donated through a grant by the Avalon Corporation to the U.S. Department of the Interior. It is now under the management of the National Park Service.

Here on the grounds of Hampton is an authentic segment of early Maryland. The formal garden and the house with its stuccoed walls and fine interior date from the years immediately following the American Revolution and are among the best examples of early Americana to be found on the continent.

In 1745, Charles Ridgely (called "the Merchant" to distinguish him from the many others of that name in the Ridgely line) purchased the property of "Northampton," a 1,500-acre tract in Baltimore County. The land was well north of the existing Tidewater settlements and into the wilderness. By 1750 Charles Ridgely owned more than seven thousand acres of Baltimore County, mostly north of Towson, the present county seat. The property included a profitable iron works and a limestone quarry which increased the wealth of the Ridgelys through two subsequent wars, the American Revolution and the Civil War.

In 1783, the same year that America's peace treaty with England was ratified, Charles Ridgely's son, Charles "the Builder," started the house at Hampton. Built in the popular Georgian style with native materials and an impressive "doom" or dome, it is thought to have been designed by a local architect and carpenter, Jehu Howell. Charles the Builder, however, did not live to enjoy it. He died only six months after it was completed in 1790. Captain Ridgely was childless and willed his estate to his nephew, Charles Ridgely Carnan, with the stipulation that the young man change his

Above: This parterre illustrates the goal of the owners of Hampton to return the estate to its original pre-1800 plan.

Left: Over forty graceful urns decorate the gardens. Originally they were to take the place of a balustrade to the terraces.

name to Charles Ridgely and take up the Ridgely coat of arms. It was this Charles Ridgely that brought Hampton to its height of beauty and renown, adding gardens and other landscaping as well as good fields of corn and wheat and a stable of fine racing horses, all supported mainly by the iron works. Charles Carnan Ridgely served as Governor of the State of Maryland from 1815 to 1818. According to Richard Parkinson, a famed traveler of the day, Ridgely, "kept the best table in America." The great hall at Hampton saw many banquets and parties with sometimes as many as three hundred guests.

Early in 1784 Charles Ridgely, the Builder, received word from Robert Ballard of an indentured Irishman, Daniel Healy, who was an expert gardener. The papers of indenture recommended Healy as a "Master of his Trade . . . . If you have a garden to make, he is worth a great deal of money to you." By the end of that year Healy was turned over to Colonel Ridgely. It is thought that he probably began to plant the garden shortly after the house was completed. Healy's work was carried on after 1795 by William Booth, an English florist and nurseryman who was hired to lay out several gardens around Baltimore.

The gardens, laid out at Hampton in the early 1800's, were in the customary formal design of the period. Three pairs of terraced gardens sloped down from a broad lawn or bowling green bordered with native cedars. A kitchen herb garden stood to the east of the

Opposite: Over 100,000 tulips are set in large drifts. Artistic groupings of colors are as outstanding as the tulips themselves.

Before anything is planted at Sherwood, all the soil is dug to a depth of two feet and replaced with good leaf mold.

The Baltimore Sunpapers

The formula that John Sherwood and his gardeners developed is not complicated, but it can be expensive. Before planting anything, all the soil is dug to a depth of two feet and replaced with good leaf mold. Each year a ton of new leaf mold and a ton of complete plant food is added. All the plants are pruned and sprayed as needed. All of the bulbs are replaced each year. The old ones go to local schools, churches and hospitals. The final technique, which Sherwood often cited as the most important, was to love everything growing in the garden. The success of the total program can readily be seen in the lasting beauty here.

The azaleas of Sherwood Gardens are second only to the bright Dutch tulips in popularity. Among the many varieties are several fragrant Dutch Ghent azalea and Asian hybrids. The lavender hues of *Lediflora rosea* and the delicate white of *Japonica alba* are beautifully combined with the pink and mauve of other varieties.

One of the favorite areas is the Bride's Garden, planted entirely in white tulips, pansies and other white flowers, against a background of dark evergreens. Many weddings have been held here among the flowers, a tradition that was begun after the sign "Bride's Garden" was first put up. One day a young couple came to him and asked if they could be married there. Although he did not know them Sherwood agreed, and helped make the wedding arrangements.

The beauty of Sherwood Gardens has been celebrated in many books and magazines over the years. At one time, Herbert Archer of the Eastman-Kodak Company had two of his photographs of the Gardens enlarged into an eighteen-by-sixty-foot mural and placed in New York's Grand Central Station for the enjoyment of thousands of commuters.

That the guests at Sherwood Gardens still consider it uniquely their own can be seen in their protective attitude during its yearly burst of bloom. Many people return year after year to enjoy the flowers. Neighbors in the vicinity of Highfield Road cheerfully put up with the annual stream of traffic and an occasional unexpected visitor to their own gardens.

The real test of the Gardens' appeal came in 1966 after Mr. Sherwood's death. That the public should lose access to this beautiful garden proved unthinkable. The city agreed to take over the job of planting the tulip bulbs and setting out the annuals each year. The new owner of the mansion and principal garden, Dr. Pedro S. de Borja, and the Neighborhood Association of which he is a member, assumed responsibility for maintenance of the flowers, shrubberies and lawns. It honors the name of John W. Sherwood who not only opened his grounds to the public for over thirty years, but loaned his art collection to the city's museums, aided the work of the Baltimore Symphony Orchestra and played an important role in solving state and local conservation problems. Sherwood Gardens is open to the public free of charge each spring for as long as the flowers are in bloom.

Gottscho-Schleisner, Inc.

Somerville, New Jersey

DUKE GARDENS

A Gathering of Fine Gardens

The Chinese Garden is filled with the delicate green of bamboo, blossoming camellias and the pink and white of lotus.

Opposite: Ornate fountains and statuary in the Italian Garden at Duke Gardens are a reminder of such elaborate places as Villa d'Este, Boboli and Villa Lante.

For the aficionado of world gardening, no more rewarding spot could be found than Duke Gardens in Somerville, New Jersey. The Gardens, started by Miss Doris Duke on the family's 2,500-acre estate, were opened to the public in 1964 and have since proved so popular that the public viewing hours have been practically doubled. Here in the Duke Gardens, under an acre of glass, there are eleven interconnected greenhouses with individually controlled climates to accommodate representative gardens of the world. The gardens vary in climate from the dryness of an Arizona desert to the lushness of a tropical jungle. In an eighty-minute tour, one can see the typical flora of England, France, Italy, Japan, China and even ancient Persia, and find flowers that are always in bloom regardless of outside temperatures. This distinguished garden is, in its way, a living history of the subject. Each separate area is planted with scrupulous attention to authenticity. Because of this, as well as the care lavished on the gardens and its outstanding regular displays, experts acclaim it the most beautiful indoor collection of plants in America.

In the Italian Garden, graceful, decorative trees rise to a height of thirty feet over plantings of jacaranda, bottle brush and acacias. South African Dombeya trees *(Dombeya wallichii),* with their heart-shaped velvety leaves and pendulous, dense clusters of scarlet flowers, add bright color and dramatic impact. Ornate fountains and statuary in the Italian Garden are a reminder that the elaborate gardens of Italy, such as the Villa d'Este, Boboli, Tivoli and Villa Lante, included the works of such artists and architects as Bartommeo Ammanati, Giambologna and Michelangelo. Plantings of lantanas and Transvaal daisies *(Gerbera jamesonii)* grace its paths.

Adjacent to the Italian Garden is the Edwardian Conservatory, a garden under glass, typical of England at the turn of the century. The graceful fronds of ferns and palms, augmented by the richly patterned curved foliage of bromeliads form a lacy filigree against the glass walls and ceiling. A choice selection of more than forty varieties of beautiful orchids is also on display.

Elsewhere on the estate, in a separate greenhouse, is a magnificent display of some twenty thousand orchids. This collection, begun by Miss Duke's father, the late James B. Duke, is considered to be one of the country's finest.

The French Garden is displayed on two levels with a high latticed canopy spanning the whole. The garden, designed in the style of Louis XVI, is patterned after one of the châteaux at Versailles.

Above: More stylized than the Chinese Garden, the Japanese Garden makes simple and symbolic use of water, rock, earth and trees.

Opposite: A high latticed canopy spans the sculptured French parterre garden at Duke. An eighteenth-century marble statue from France is at each end of the garden.

From the upper level one looks down at a large parterre in a *fleur-de-lis* design planted with low-growing Japanese holly and colorful red, white and blue petunias. The parterre was an important concept in formal garden design. It was introduced by the French with the building of the gardens at the Tuileries. The old square parquet garden was replaced by ornamental *parterres de broderie.* Terraces were created above them to better reveal the designs on the ground. Flower color was augmented by the colors of sand, brick and coal dust, and by the clay that was used for the paths and to fill the spaces between flowers.

French eighteenth-century marble statues at each end of the garden are flanked by urns filled with white lilies *(Lilium candidum).* Along the walls are trees of privet *(Ligustrum vulgare)* trained as standards, and hanging baskets of geraniums.

The English Garden has the intimate informal charm so typical of that land of garden-lovers. A brick path leads through its four separate aspects: a topiary garden, a garden of summer flowers, an

Above: One of four different aspects of the English Garden is this curious sundial display featuring small succulent plants.

Right: In the Arizona Desert Garden, short spiny pincushion and tall *Cereus* cacti grow in a sandy replica of a true desert.

154

Elizabethan Knot Garden and a succulent garden in a sundial design. The fine art of topiary was brought to its apex by the British. They worked with slow-growing evergreens, such as yews, and sheared them into various geometric and fantastic shapes. At Duke the topiary work takes the form of several amusing animals.

The English took great pleasure in domesticating their native wildflowers. The summer garden here includes the delicate colors of foxgloves, columbine, violets, primroses, daisies and other traditional favorites. In the Elizabethan Knot Garden, twenty-five varieties of herbs form an elaborately and intricately entwined pattern. The Knot Garden first appeared in England at the beginning of the sixteenth century with intricate patterning of pot herbs such as thyme, hyssop, rosemary, sage and thrift.

The Chinese Garden reveals the special splendor of the gardens of the Orient. Marco Polo, the famed early traveler to China, marveled at the number of magnificent gardens he saw there. In the following centuries the ancient culture of China contributed in many ways to the gardens of the West. At Duke Gardens the Chinese Garden is entered through a grove of variegated bamboo that opens to a large pool. Bamboo, a symbol of longevity, was one of the most important plantings in any Chinese garden. An arched stone bridge leads across the pool to a small pavilion. The garden is filled with the delicate green of bamboo, blossoming camellias, bright calceolaria and the pink and white of the lovely lotus.

Tropical tuberoses, plumeria and jasmine grow in the Persian Garden, where a brick walk leads along both sides of a reflecting pool.

Photos: Gottscho-Schleisner, Inc.

At the far end of the garden is a latticed pergola covered with clusters of purple wisteria and camellias. The Chinese Gardens, unlike the gardens of the West, were not designed in monumental scale or strict symmetry. They tended instead toward the beauty of simplicity and naturalness. This character is revealed by the one at Duke Gardens.

More stylized than the Chinese Garden, but a natural descendent of Chinese tradition, is the Japanese garden with its commandingly simple and symbolic use of water, rock, earth and trees. The Japanese Garden at the Duke Conservatory reflects traditional uses of water and living plants in a design that captures the tranquil beauty for which such gardens are world renowned.

Perhaps the most outstanding display is the Persian Garden, a replica of designs found in seventeenth-century Persia where so much of garden tradition first began. The ancient Persians found the parks of Assyria and Babylonia so beautiful to behold that they set out to re-create them in their own country. The art of planting trees was taught to Persian youths along with skill at forging armor. Through the centuries, the gardens of Persia became so lovely that the Greeks, with the rise of their own culture, attempted to emulate them. The Greek word "paradise" derives from the Persian *pardes*, or park.

In the Persian Garden, a double brick path leads along both sides of a seventy-six-foot reflecting pool. At the end of the path sits a *chabutra*, or raised platform pavilion. Beyond this pavilion, brick steps lead to a fountain waterway and four sunken beds of roses. Roses were greatly admired by the Persians who loved them growing in the garden and as a motif in artistic design. Tropical tuberoses, plumeria and jasmine are also included in the Persian Garden beneath stone mogul grilles and arches.

From Persia the visitor enters the Jungle Garden where an earthen path winds past gnarled trees, huge boulders, a shallow stream and two waterfalls. So realistic is the setting that we almost expect the call of wild birds or the cry of a jungle animal from behind a tall palm or sinuous vine. This lush planting of exotics includes pandanus, mangoes, bananas, water lilies, tropical orchids and a fine collection of philodendron.

The Arizona Desert Garden reveals the opposite side of the spectrum with cacti and other succulents native to the American Southwest. Cactus varieties, from the short spiny *Mammillarias* or pincushion cactus to the tall *Cereus* with its attractive flowers and succulents such as yucca, agave and the aloe, grow here in a sandy replica of the true desert.

In addition to the display gardens, Duke Gardens has other greenhouses where all the new flowering material is grown. A full-time staff of forty horticulturists, gardeners and maintenance men work to keep the Gardens in bloom the year around. With its capsule view of garden beauty from Italy to England and from the Orient to the dry desert, few are the places where an hour or so could be spent more pleasurably or informatively than in a tour of this unique display.

Opposite: Magnificent floral displays offer
a riot of color in each of the eleven
scrupulously authentic gardens.

Above: So realistic is the setting of the
Jungle Garden that one expects the call of
wild birds or the cry of a jungle animal.

Below: The Edwardian Conservatory, typical
of England at the turn of the century,
offers a choice selection of orchids.

Independence National Historical Park, Philadelphia, Pennsylvania
AN EIGHTEENTH-CENTURY GARDEN
A Small and Charming Garden in an Historic Setting

An Eighteenth-Century Garden opened in 1966 and in that first year volunteers contributed five hundred hours of labor.

Philadelphia in the late seventeenth and early eighteenth centuries was not only the second largest city in the British Empire, but was also an important center of horticultural interest and activity. Thomas Jefferson wrote in 1807 to his friend Dr. Caspar Wistar, for whom the American wisteria was named, that he wished his fifteen-year-old grandson could be educated in botany at the Woodlands in Philadelphia since, "there are particular branches of science, which are not so advantageously taught anywhere else in the United States as in Philadelphia." The first professor of botany in the United States began the country's first botany department in 1763 at the University of Pennsylvania. And such famous plantsmen as William Penn, John and William Bartram, Francis Daniel Pastorius (founder of Germantown) and Benjamin Franklin conducted their botanical researches from the Philadelphia area and vied with one another for the best American and foreign specimens.

In 1827 the Pennsylvania Horticultural Society, one of the oldest such organizations in the country, was founded in Philadelphia by George Pepper, Mathew Carey, Joseph Hopkins and others for the purpose of "promoting and encouraging horticulture by the growth of vegetables, plants, trees, fruits, and flowers." Many Philadelphians of the time had gardens, and in Germantown, and on the acres along the Schuylkill River, gardens of considerable size flourished. The membership of the Horticultural Society steadily increased until declining abruptly during the disorders brought on by the American Civil War. The organization survived, however, and after the war it began to grow again.

The headquarters of the Pennsylvania Horticultural Society are now located at 325 Walnut Street in Philadelphia's Independence National Historical Park. This is the site of Independence Hall and a replica of an eighteenth-century garden sponsored by the Society. In this park, echoing with memories of historic events, the little Garden sparkles like a jewel against the muted red brick and wrought iron of buildings dating from the colonial period.

How the Garden came to grow here is a story in itself. As the old buildings in Independence Park were renovated, the National Park Service was faced with the problem of finding tenants whose history was directly connected with eighteenth-century Philadelphia. Although the Pennsylvania Horticultural Society does not immediately fit these qualifications, it has an older companion organization, the Philadelphia Society for Promoting Agriculture, which was founded in 1785 and does qualify. The two organizations were

Located in Independence National Historical Park in
Philadelphia, the little garden sparkles like
a jewel against the muted red brick and wrought
iron of buildings dating from the colonial period.

Above: Near the Garden stands Independence Hall, completed about 1748, the work of Andrew Hamilton and Edmund Woolley.

Below: Surrounded by neat hedges of green cushion holly, four lantanas brighten the Garden with their compact blossoms.

offered joint quarters in three old shops in the Park, originally occupied by Dr. William Chandler, an apothecary, Robert Kid, a copper merchant, and William Fling, a cabinetmaker. Surrounded by Independence Hall, Carpenter's Hall, the Philadelphia Exchange and other historic buildings, the horticultural organizations assumed their rightful place.

Between the new offices and buildings at 4th and Walnut (which originally belonged to John Todd, the first husband of Dolley Madison) there is a small plot of land, said to have been the garden of colonist William Hamilton. Here the Pennsylvania Horticultural Society agreed to create an eighteenth-century garden, similar to the one that Hamilton himself might have grown. The agreement between the Society and the National Park Service stated that the Park Service would install the permanent plantings if the Horticultural Society would plant flowers and maintain the garden and buildings to preserve the historic atmosphere.

An Eighteenth-Century Garden opened in 1966. In that first year, members of the Pennsylvania Horticultural Society spent more than five hundred hours of volunteer labor, planting and working the Garden, an accomplishment which earned for them the praise of Mrs. Lyndon B. Johnson. She said at the dedication, "Members of the Pennsylvania Horticultural Society have volunteered long hours of nurturing this garden, clipping, weeding, and doing countless nameless tasks that have assured its lasting beauty. Seldom can public park agencies afford such constant care, . . . [this] gift of talent is a priceless benefit."

Around the brick walls of the Garden the shrubs that were popular in the eighteenth century lend a sense of maturity as well as history to the Garden. Here are the blossoms of cockspur hawthorn *(Crataegus crus-galli),* bayberry *(Myrica pennsylvanica),* the sweet pepperbush *(Clethra alnifolia),* holly and such old-fashioned roses as Souvenir de la Malmaison and Alfred de Dalmas. Sixteen small parterres bordered with graveled walks are the permanent setting for an ever-changing display of colorful flowers.

After careful thought, discussion and research, the Garden Committee of the Pennsylvania Horticultural Society decided that, although the eighteenth-century gardener would have obtained for his garden the best and most colorful plant specimens he could, these same flowers and shrubs might appear drab and uninteresting to the average visitor to Independence Park. Therefore, instead of planting the original specimens of these early flowers, they have used the more colorful modern hybrids of the same plants.

Each year 1,300 tulips in fifty-seven different varieties are donated by The Netherlands Flower Bulb Institute in appreciation of the Society's maintaining this remarkable garden in the heart of a once blighted area. The tulips are planted throughout the Garden, and are followed by a colorful display of annuals — pink geraniums, zinnias, ageratums, heliotrope, nicotiana and salvia — all in full bloom. As is required to maintain the color, these flowers are replaced by more than eight hundred snapdragons or other annuals

Courtesy Pennsylvania Horticultural Society

in bloom. As fall approaches, a brilliant display of chrysanthemums floods the Garden. The rectangular plot is flanked by a number of fine young trees including a Washington thorn *(Crataegus phaeno-pyrum)*, dogwood and a ginkgo.

In addition to An Eighteenth-Century Garden, the Society maintains two other plantings here. Beyond the delicate white lattice work of a gazebo is a tiny orchard which was common to eighteenth-century gardens. Carpeted with a lawn of Merion bluegrass, the orchard includes grapes, as well as apples and pears, and is a welcome retreat for weary and footsore visitors. The third section is an attractive vegetable, herb and cutting garden which is not always open to the public.

Few gardens are so strategically placed, as this one near Independence Hall, to produce in its visitors the optimum of delighted surprise. Here, in the heart of a large city, surrounded by buildings steeped in the history of our nation, is a small and charming place with flowers and fragrances familiar to anyone who has ever grown a garden.

Above left: As fall approaches, a brilliant display of chrysanthemums floods the Garden with many different colors.

Above right: This careful copy of an eighteenth-century gazebo is thickly covered with vines of Concord grape.

HERSHEY ROSE GARDENS AND ARBORETUM

A Famous Public Rose Garden in the Lebanon Valley

This *Boy with Leaking Boot* is one of
twenty-three identical statues in the world, all
presumably created by one unidentified artist.

Opposite: Late spring at Hershey brings a
spectacular showing of some thirty thousand
tulips of more than five hundred varieties.

The enticing odor of good chocolate is not the only aroma in the
air of "The Chocolate Town," Hershey, Pennsylvania. There is also
the fragrance of roses, for one of the largest rose gardens in the
country grows here.

Milton S. Hershey began his career as a maker of caramel candies
in Lancaster, Pennsylvania, before the turn of the century. The
quality of his wares was soon recognized, and by 1903 he
established the town of Hershey for his chocolate factory and the
people who worked there. From the beginning, Mr. Hershey had the
idea of a town filled with parks and community centers, gardens
and playgrounds, for he believed in the value of a beautiful
community. The grounds around his own home were planted with
roses, peonies and other popular flowers of the day, and the large
rambling Hotel Hershey, which he built, was a frequent meeting
place for local flower and garden associations.

In April 1936, Mr. Hershey was invited to a conference dinner of
the Garden Club Federation of Pennsylvania being held at the
Hotel. There he was asked by Dr. J. Horace McFarland, a well-
known printer of horticultural books and owner of one of the All-
America Rose Test gardens, for a contribution of one million dollars
to help establish a National Rosarium to be built near Washington,
D.C. Mr. Hershey proposed instead his own plan to establish a rose
garden at Hershey, and suggested that if the Garden Club had that
kind of money in mind they ought to consider spending some of it
there in Pennsylvania. "We'll build our own gardens first," Mr.
Hershey said, "and see what happens."

Before the conference was over, it was announced that a public
rose garden would soon be started in Hershey. Work started almost
immediately. The site was an attractive three-and-one-half-acre plot
just south of Hotel Hershey, near a circular grove of trees which
was left to grow because of a property line dispute between
previous owners. Under the supervision of Harry L. Erdman,
manager of Hershey's landscape division, plans were drawn and
construction was begun that summer. There was an erosion gully
through the plot, and this was developed as a reservoir for storm
waters to provide water for irrigation, and as a scenic feature of the
garden. Water pipes and electric conduits were laid. The beds were
graded and prepared. By late August, the garden was ready for fall

This statue, *Rebecca with Water Jug,*
was cast in Italy by an
unknown but talented craftsman.

planting. More than twelve thousand roses in 112 varieties were set out by early November of the same year.

The garden was opened to the public in late May of 1937. The first weekend in June, with the roses in full and impressive bloom, there were more than twenty thousand visitors in a single day. By the end of the season more than 200,000 people had seen the garden.

Mr. Hershey was so pleased with the public's interest that he resolved to enlarge the garden. In 1937, seven thousand roses were added, and the following year four thousand more. This brought the total number of plants to 23,000 and the number of different varieties to seven hundred.

Today, this is one of the finest rose gardens to be found. In the acres of terraced beds there are 42,000 rose bushes in 1,200 varieties and in every shade and color from pure red, white and yellow, to delicate orange, salmon, pale yellow and even shades of lavender. There are all the types: hybrid teas, climbers, polyanthas, floribundas, hybrid perpetuals and grandifloras.

The pond that was once an erosion ditch is now Swan Lake, with thousands of gold fish, a family of swans and other water birds. From one to four cygnets are born each year to the swans on the lake who mate and stay here for life. A ground cover of beautiful Mermaid roses with their single cup-shaped blooms of clear yellow surrounds the lake.

Along All-America Avenue, roses which have been awarded the honor line the pathway. Here are the pink-tinged ivory of the variety called Peace, Miss All-American Beauty with soft pink blooms, the orange-red glow of Tropicana, and all the rest of the great roses that have earned this coveted award down through the years. Around a peaceful grove of oak trees where Mr. Hershey loved to sit on cool summer evenings, there is now a large planting of the M.S. Hershey rose. This hardy variety was named for him by the Coddington Rose Growers of New Jersey.

In the Garden of Old-fashioned Roses are the time-tested beauties that grandmother might have grown. Here we find huge bushes of Crested Moss with pink crests like Napoleon's tri-cornered hat, the Damask Rose, Harrison's Yellow and bushes and trellises of fragrant favorites. The Rose Test Garden grows the newest of American roses, many of them as yet unnamed, and identified only by serial numbers.

Around Imperial Pool, which supplements the Gardens' irrigation system as well as the facilities for swans and ducks, the beautiful crimson red of massed Chrysler Imperial roses is reflected in the quiet waters. Throughout the garden the roses continue their colorful bloom from early June until the end of October.

In 1941, by which time more than a half million people were visiting the Gardens annually, Mr. Hershey decided to add seventeen acres of adjoining farmland. The local farmers had declared the land absolutely worthless for growing farm crops. In the autumn of the same year it was planted with trees, shrubs, annuals, perennials and bulbs.

Left: Some of the many tulip beds are whimsically arranged to resemble a windmill, a wooden shoe or a tulip.

Below: The striking white of a picket fence and wrought-iron benches contrasts with green and the myriad colors of roses.

In the spring, there is a show of more than 150 varieties of narcissus, and 40 varieties of hyacinths. Anemones, calathus, crocus, scilla and muscari cover the seventeen acres of garden land, blending with the bloom of hundreds of flowering shrubs and trees including dogwood, redbud, azalea, lilac, magnolia, spirea, forsythia and rhododendron.

The peak of the season, from mid-April to mid-May, brings a spectacular showing of some thirty thousand tulips. Some are whimsically arranged in beds that resemble a windmill, a wooden shoe or a tulip. More than five hundred varieties from the standard, colorful breeder and cottage types to the variegated beauty of the parrot tulips are represented here. A giant display of five thousand chrysanthemums, including All-America selections and new giant Harvest Mums, brightens the perennial beds all through the fall.

In summer the flower garden is a quiet shaded place, accented by the color and fragrance of hydrangeas and mock orange and hundreds of perennials. After the tulips are lifted from their beds, some fourteen thousand annuals are put in to replace them.

Mr. Hershey appreciated and understood the stabilizing influence of large native trees. Throughout the twenty-three-acre garden, the beautiful old oaks, elms, maples, beech, birch, poplars and other hardwoods and numerous evergreens have been preserved in groves and as single specimens. Where new plantings were required to enhance the design of the garden, the best of ornamental shrubs and trees were chosen. Three magnificent California redwood *(Sequoia sempervirens)* are planted here. Along All-American Avenue, stately incense cedars *(Libocedrus decurrens)* overlook the blooming roses. Here, too, are specimen Lebanon cedars *(C. libani)* as well as the tall Atlantic blue cedars that closely resemble the Cedars of Lebanon except for the bluish color of the needles. The graceful, golden chain tree *(Laburnum anagyroides)* with its pendulous golden blossoms, is another fine tree for visitors to see and consider planting in their own gardens. Behind the hotel, acres of untouched woodlands provide a bird sanctuary and wildlife preserve.

From the hill overlooking the rainbow colors of the garden and the fertile Lebanon Valley, listening to the soft chimes of the Memorial Carillon, one can only be glad that Milton Hershey decided to keep his one million dollars and invest his time, money and effort in the creation of a garden in his own name.

Above: More than five hundred varieties of tulips from the breeder and cottage types to the variegated parrot tulips are represented.

Below: Along All-America Avenue, one finds the pink-tinged ivory of the variety called Peace and the orange-red glow of Tropicana.

Above: Mr. Hershey appreciated and understood
the stabilizing influence of native trees,
such as this grove of birches.

Left: Hundreds of flowering shrubs and trees
including dogwood, redbud, lilac, spirea,
forsythia and rhododendron decorate the area.

167

Kennett Square, Pennsylvania

LONGWOOD GARDENS

European Grandeur and American Informality

This spiral piece in the Yew and Topiary Garden shows the strong influence of English formality on American gardens.

Opposite: Longwood combines the grandeur of European gardens with the informality of woodland gardens in their natural habitat.

One of the most remarkable estates in this country is Longwood Gardens, beautifully situated on a thousand acres of hills and woodlands near Kennett Square, Pennsylvania. Longwood, developed by the late Pierre S. du Pont, offers the grandeur of the best European formal gardens — green hedges, colorful flower borders, sparkling fountains — in combination with America's greatest contribution to gardening — informal woodland gardens with shrubs, flowers and trees in their natural habitat.

Impressive both for its size and variety of plants, Longwood Gardens also has a noble history dating from 1700 when William Penn conveyed this part of the rolling Pennsylvania countryside to his friend and fellow Quaker, George Peirce. The Battle of the Brandywine, one of the first battles in the American Revolution, was fought a short distance from the site of the present Gardens. During the American Civil War the Peirce estate was used as a station in the famous Underground Railway, providing shelter for many runaway slaves. When the war ended, part of the estate was used as a Quaker headquarters and it was then that the property first took its name from the long wooded strip nearby. The Peirce family home, built in 1730, is currently used as an administration building for the Gardens.

Many of the fine old trees seen here were planted for the Peirce arboretum by twin brothers, Joshua and Samuel Peirce. Here one can see 150-170-year-old English yews, copper beeches, paulownia, cucumber magnolias, Kentucky coffee-trees *(Gymnocladus dioica)* and an immense ginkgo tree measuring three and a half feet across its trunk, that was among the first of this ancient species ever to be brought to America. This part of the Peirce estate, known as "Peirce's Park," had been open to the public since 1800. In fact, the trees marked for cutting were what caught Mr. du Pont's attention during a Sunday drive in 1906 and prompted him to buy the land as the site of his planned estate.

Pierre S. du Pont, the financial wizard of the du Pont empire and General Motors, was a simple, unassuming man with a lifelong interest in horticulture, music and drama. As early as 1921 the du Ponts opened their magnificent conservatories to the public. Since that time more than seven million visitors have seen the collection of tree ferns and other tender plants in the elegant garden setting.

In 1925, after visiting Italy's beautiful water gardens, Mr. du Pont began the first of Longwood's famous fountains, the Italian Water Garden. It was based on the design of the original at the Florentine

A. Devaney, Inc. N.Y.

Gottscho-Schleisner, Inc.

Above: The Conservatory Auditorium features Australian and Mexican tree ferns.

Opposite: To the rear of the main conservatories are thirteen Water Lily Pools. This one contains the South American water platter, a fascinating plant.

Villa Gamberaia. This intriguing display of the many ways that water can be used in the garden is often missed by visitors because of its location at the far north end of the woodland.

Pierre du Pont spent so much time at work in his gardens that he was often mistaken for one of the gardeners. He also supervised the construction of the estate's many fountains. The Fountain Garden, with its aura of Old World tranquility, is built of cut-stonework purchased in Italy. The Main Water Garden, which lies just south of the central conservatory, is designed on two levels and includes an elaborate series of fountains, basins and canals. From mid-May to mid-October the fountains sparkle three evenings each week for a spectacular half-hour display of color that has been likened to "liquid fireworks."

In addition to its more elaborate fountains, many of the other gardens at Longwood are built around fountains and pools. The cooling sound of splashing water follows the visitor from one display to the next. In the Water Lily Pools, behind the central conservatory, these crisp, bright flowers rise from the water and bloom from July to October. There are also lotuses, water hyacinths, rushes and other water plants to be seen here. In the largest of the pools is the exotic South American water platter *(Victoria amazonica),* one of the most fascinating of all water lilies. Two large

The three and a half acres of greenhouses contain a marvelous variety, ranging from exotic tropical plants to common house plants.

Opposite: In the main conservatory, massive vine-covered columns add to the feeling of natural spaciousness.

natural lakes, one with a huge planting of daffodils on the shore, and a waterfall flanked by dogwoods and evergreens, complete the series of fountains and lakes.

Since 1946 the Longwood Foundation, a nonprofit philanthropic organization, has managed the Gardens. The present director of the Gardens, Dr. R.J. Seibert, carefully carries on the du Pont tradition of conservation and improvement. Wherever possible the fine old trees from the original Peirce estate have been preserved. These include many evergreen — yew, box, spruce, pine and hemlock, as well as magnolia, ginkgo, bald cypress and beech. The Longwood Foundation has also made several additions to the Gardens.

Due to the lay of the land in Pennsylvania's gently rolling hills and to the imaginative placement of plants, the formal gardens, three and a half acres of greenhouse, informal landscaped gardens, fountains and the arboretum itself spaciously cover the grounds without any feeling of crowding. A walk along the Gardens' paths leads in and out of formal and informal settings and is memorable for its liquid change of mood, tone and color.

Among the formal settings are a rose garden with 150 different varieties including the rose, 'Mrs. Pierre S. du Pont,' the analemmatic sundial, and the famous topiary garden, an excellent example of this traditional art with yew trees carefully trimmed to the shape of birds, animals and other fantastic creatures. The informal gardens include the waterfall with its plantings of dogwood and evergreen, paths thickly carpeted with fragrant pine needles, a woodland garden where a variety of charming plants bloom throughout the season. In the arboretum there are places that seem as untamed as the original woodlands. The tall trees blend with the surrounding wooded hills, making the garden appear to stretch for miles past its border.

The annual "Calendar of Flowering" is as dependable as nature herself. Beginning with camellias, cherry blossoms and daffodils in April, it is followed by lilac, forsythia and magnolia in early May. Then come the masses of rhododendron and azaleas, dogwood and wisteria. In June there are late azaleas, the beauty bush and the fragrant mock orange. Late summer brings buddleia, crape myrtle, the silk tree and Franklinia. These are followed by the first of the *Camellia sasanqua* varieties which bloom in October, and the later ones which continue until the November frosts. And, of course, there are the brilliant beds of annuals and perennials every season.

Longwood's three and a half acres of greenhouses, considered by many even more impressive than the outdoor gardens, contain a marvelous variety, ranging from the most exotic tropical plants to the most common of house plants. There is an unrivaled display of orchids enriched by bequests from the famed collection of the late Mrs. William K. du Pont, a noted fancier of the intriguing plant. There is a desert house with American cacti, yuccas and century plants, as well as bizarre plants from the African desert. In the conservatories are mature specimens of such tropical fruits as bananas, oranges, annonas and lemons. But, in the tradition of Mr. du Pont, who believed that conservatories should also include specimens of garden and house plants, much of the greenhouse area

is devoted to azaleas, tulips, rhododendron, geraniums and other showy plants handsomely grouped and labeled for the benefit of home gardeners. The main conservatory with its high ceiling and sunken garden areas has great architectural charm. The massive columns, like tree trunks covered with creeping vines, flank the indoor lawn and add to the feeling of natural spaciousness.

In addition to the year-round horticultural displays, which are the main attraction, the Longwood Foundation offers a variety of public events and services. At the Singing Chimes tower in the center of the Gardens, there are regular carillon concerts throughout the year. Summer brings benefit performances sponsored by outside organizations to Longwood's Open Air Theatre. The amphitheatre has a sixty-two-foot stage, large underground dressing rooms, and it seats 2,100 people. It also features a unique replacement for the typical theatre curtain — a sheet of water that spurts up from a trough in front of the stage. Hedges form the wings, and tall trees serve as the backdrop.

Special concerts are often played on the huge pipe organ in the main conservatory. Mr. du Pont had this magnificent instrument built for the evenings when he would play it for his wife's enjoyment. It is one of the largest in all America.

During the winter months there is a regular series of lectures given by experts in many fields of horticulture and botany. For those fortunate enough to live within driving distance of the Gardens, there are short courses on many subjects that the home gardener might fancy.

With the beauty and variety of its gardens and the diversified cultural aspects of its programs, Longwood is gaining a well-deserved reputation in the world of horticulture, garden design and theatre arts, as a significant national center.

A. Devaney, Inc., N.Y.

Gottscho-Schleisner, Inc.

Above: The famed Fountain Garden, with its aura of Old World tranquility, features "cubed" maples and basins made of stone from Italy.

Opposite: Except for the plant materials and fountains, the Italian Water Garden is a replica of a water garden at the Villa Gamberaia near Florence, Italy.

Left: The brilliant shades of the borders are accented by lush green turf and young trees in full foliage.

Elizabethtown, New York

THE COLONIAL GARDEN

Retreat in the Adirondacks

Elizabethtown, situated in the Adirondack Mountains of New York, is a town interested in history. Perhaps it is because this village, with its broad, tree-lined streets, old brick courthouse, white frame houses and unchanging store fronts, reflects the quiet loveliness of another era. Or perhaps it is because of the ageless beauty of the surrounding mountains, or because of the history made by the early settlers, by Indian raids, by runaway slaves who stayed here when the town was a stop on the Underground Railroad. The pre-Civil War State Senator, Augustus C. Hand, grandfather of two eminent members of the United States Circuit Court of Appeals, August N. Hand and Learned Hand, was a citizen of this community.

The Colonial Garden, on the grounds of the Adirondack Center, the museum of the Essex County Historical Society, in Elizabethtown, exemplifies the local interest in history. The idea for a garden was suggested by two summer residents of the nearby village of Lewis who offered to help the Essex County Historical Society design an authentic colonial garden. Mr. and Mrs. Ira M. Younker had visited the gardens of Henry VIII at Hampton Court in England and came back with the belief that some of the historical landscape in our own country should be preserved.

The concept was approved and several members of the Essex County Historical Society and a landscape architect worked with Mr. and Mrs. Younker to design the garden which, when opened in 1956, incorporated the best features of colonial and eighteenth-century gardens. Today the Garden is a miniature, jewel-like retreat. Encircled by the wooded slopes of the Adirondacks, with Mount Raven forming a near-perfect backdrop, the Colonial Garden is patterned after the sunken garden at Hampton Court. To achieve the proper effect, the flower border around the central plot of grass is raised by seven inches, and at the rear of the Garden, the grade is eleven inches higher than the central rectangle. The plot is divided by graveled paths edged with brick in a style popular in the gardens of the eighteenth century.

In the raised beds, favorite flowers of colonial days reach their peak of bloom in July and August. Brilliant masses of cineraria *(Senecio cruentus),* tall spikes of delphinium, the verbena, dianthus, phlox, dwarf cockscomb *(Celosia cristata),* peonies, heliotrope, columbine, foxglove, primulas, forget-me-nots, marigolds, pink and lavender petunias are planted here for an ever-changing series of color combinations that are beautiful from early spring to late fall.

The unsullied white of a graceful urn post almost glows against the sky and the majestic backdrop of the Adirondack Mountains.

Opposite: The embossed lead cistern and dolphin at the Colonial Garden are each nearly two centuries old. Lead was the characteristic garden metal in England at one time.

Above: The sundial of Portland stone is an eighteenth-century piece brought from Kirkby Mallory Hall near Leicester, England.

The Colonial Garden shares with all formal plantings the advantage of not losing its beauty during the winter months. The symmetry of the beds is revealed even when the ground is covered with snow.

The many structures and ornaments in the Garden illustrate the careful planning and attention to authenticity that make it such a pleasure to visit. The entrance is through a handsome gate that is a reproduction of one built in 1760 at the Pepperell House in Kittery, Maine. The diamond design in the white picket fence, into which the gate is set, is copied from a fence design used by Thomas Jefferson at Monticello.

At the far end of the Garden, a sundial dominates the rectangular lawn. Made in the eighteenth century of Portland stone, the dial was once used at Kirkby Mallory Hall near Leicester, England. The brick under foot, laid out in a circular pattern, again brings Jefferson to mind, for the pattern is the same as that used at the University of Virginia in the rotunda that he is believed to have designed. Handcrafted iron benches, in the style used by George Washington at Mount Vernon, his magnificent home on the Potomac, provide places to rest and absorb the pleasant feeling of a graceful and less hectic time.

No colonial garden would be complete without a summer house. The example here, set to one side of the Garden, is a simple reproduction of a 1760 design. It has a railing of white pickets and the corners of the red roof are topped with simple white urns. On the other side of the Garden is a decorated lead cistern, dated 1776, into which flows a jet of water from a lead dolphin set into a low brick wall. These attractive pieces are from the garden at Bern Hill, Ewhurst, in Surrey, England.

The back walls of the Garden are reproductions, though reduced in scale, of the walls around the Capitol at Colonial Williamsburg. With their rounded top edge, these walls, laid in Flemish bond inside and English bond on the outside, are a fine example of early American masonry work.

Many of the details at the Colonial Garden were developed with the help of craftsmen and advisors from Colonial Williamsburg. The posts and connecting iron chain lining the approach to the Garden are reproductions of those at the Governor's Palace. These chains, as well as other iron work at the Colonial Garden, were handcrafted at Williamsburg in the manner of the colonial ironmasters.

On two sides of the Garden, cedar hedges border the dazzling display of flowers. A crew of local workmen scoured the surrounding countryside to find the most perfect cedar specimens, and these trees, from three to twelve feet tall, were carefully dug and brought from the woods to the Garden. Flowering shrubs including lilacs, Japanese quince and red-stem dogwood are combined with such evergreens as spruce, hemlock and juniper, and some fine large hardwoods to complete the Garden.

Left: The diamond design in the picket fence at the front of the Garden is copied from a fence design used by Jefferson at Monticello.

In the dense woods adjacent to the Colonial Garden, there are nature trails through the Wildflower Garden. Here, under the branches of immense trees, the forest floor is carpeted with wood sorrel, cucumber root, wild geranium, May apple, St. John's-wort, wood anemones, shooting star, mallow, red and white banberry, Canada and wood lilies, and other beautiful wildflowers that are native to this part of the Adirondacks.

In the Adirondack Center Museum, of which the Colonial Garden is a part, there are other historical displays to enjoy. Although they are not directly connected with gardening or the eighteenth century, the exhibits, by the Essex County Historical Society, include furniture, tools and other artifacts used by the early mountain settlers. Like the Garden, the Museum is steeped in history, although of a more primitive aspect, combining here both the elegance of eighteenth-century formality, and the rough tools used by the pioneers. Elizabethtown honors two revealing faces of the nation's past. This combination of vigor and appreciation of beauty is central to the American experience and should never be forgotten.

The back walls of the Garden are reproductions, reduced in scale, of the walls around the Capitol at Colonial Williamsburg.

179

Old Westbury, Long Island, New York

OLD WESTBURY GARDENS

A Great Estate Which Follows the English Style

The entrance roadway is lined with a double *allée* of little-leaf lindens brought from England in 1906 as eight-foot specimens.

Opposite: A delicate wrought-iron gate opens into Old Westbury's walled Italian Garden, where a staff of over twenty gardeners presents a constantly changing floral display.

Forty-five minutes away from the thunder of New York City traffic the quiet grounds of the former John S. Phipps estate, Old Westbury, reflect the elegance of Long Island at the turn of the century. This part of New York was then "the country" for wealthy city businessmen and financiers. On the great estates were tennis courts of the finest turf, polo grounds with stables and paddocks for the valued ponies. Old Westbury was no exception. A classic picture of Georgian elegance, the house sits serenely on a gentle rise overlooking a hundred-acre park of woodlands and gardens. The house and grounds were designed in their present style in 1905-1906 by George Crawley, the famous British architect. John Phipps was a good personal friend of Crawley and the entire estate reflects their mutual appreciation of the English style of landscape design. The land itself can be traced back to the Indians. It was purchased by Captain John Seaman from the Rockaway tribe in the seventeenth century. During the 1800's it was owned by Elias Hicks, a well-known Quaker preacher, and used as a center for the varied activities of the Quaker faith.

When Old Westbury was dedicated and opened to the public in 1959, Mrs. Etienne Phipps Boegner, a resident of the estate for the past fifty years, spoke of her father and mother and their love for gardens and parks. Her mother, Mrs. Boegner recalled, was fond of every tree and flower at Old Westbury, and hoped they would be preserved. Her father, son of Henry Phipps who was a partner to Andrew Carnegie, was a well-known businessman in his own right. He also understood the need for preservation and out of his love for this country's natural beauty he endowed several parks and wildlife preserves. Among these are Cape Hatteras Point in North Carolina; a wildlife sanctuary at Barnegat Bay, New Jersey; and in Florida, Silver Lake Boy Scout Camp in Leon County, Phipps Park at West Palm Beach and Phipps Park in Martin County. Upon his death in 1958, Mr. Phipps' will insured that Old Westbury would be established as a public garden and museum.

The entrance to the Gardens of Old Westbury is through monumental wrought-iron gates designed by the architect and a roadway lined with a double *allée* of little-leaf lindens brought from England in 1906 as eight-foot specimens. Elsewhere in the garden are similar *allées* of beech which were in the same shipment. Beyond the parking area is a curving drive with a fine view of the front of Westbury House, stately against a wide sweep of green lawn. Inside the mansion, which is a museum in itself, there is a

Gottscho-Schleisner, Inc.

Above: Occasional summer evening concerts are held on the Great South Lawn where nature's beauty and man's art are both reflected.

Right: The many sundials at Old Westbury serve as decorative accents, their whiteness contrasting with the dark green of grass.

Opposite: The terrace wall is covered with wisteria and holds busts which look out at the lushness of the Great Lawn.

A. Devaney, Inc., N.Y.

182

Courtesy New York State Department of Commerce

The giant boxwood in the Boxwood Garden
was already over a hundred years old when
it was brought from Virginia in 1931.

Opposite: The Phipps family has aimed at
creating a feeling of beauty rather than
a living textbook of botanical specimens.

The one hundred acres of land at Old Westbury
were owned during the 1800's by Elias Hicks,
a well-known Quaker preacher.

Gottscho-Schleisner, Inc.

magnificent collection of Chippendale and Wedgwood furniture.
Here, too, is one of this country's finest private collections of
paintings by English and American artists of the past two centuries.
There are beautiful works by George Morland, Simon Elwes, Sir
Joshua Reynolds, Thomas Gainsborough, John Singer Sargent, John
Constable and other fine artists of that era. Westbury's motto,
inscribed over the portal, reads, *"Pax in Troentibus — Salus
Exeuntibus"* ("Peace to those who enter, good health to those who
go out").

Turning away from the house, the path to the garden leads down
a broad flight of steps, past colorful banks of hybrid rhododendron
to a small lake where guests could once ferry themselves across in a
swan-shaped ferry boat, now elegantly at anchor in the middle of
the lake. The Boxwood Garden, in formal eighteenth-century style,
accents the far side of this lake. The charming setting was carefully
designed to provide an inviting outlook from the house. Large
specimens of English boxwood, already over one hundred years old
when they were transplanted from Virginia, outline the length of a
quiet lily pool. At the far end of this area, flanked by tall weeping
beeches, a colonnade, covered with climbing roses, shelters an
eighteenth-century terra-cotta statue of Diana the huntress.

Many of the trees in this section of the garden are very old, having
been here long before the Phipps family purchased the land. Tall
old specimens of brittle willow *(Salix fragilis)*, red maple *(Acer
rubrum)*, and Japanese white pine *(Pinus parviflora)* are listed by
the Long Island Horticultural Society as being the largest of their
species to be found in the area. Other large trees — umbrella pines,
sycamores, sweetgum and Japanese cutleaf maple — lend their cool
green shade to the area around the West Pond.

Through a border of lilac, a pathway leads from the Boxwood
Garden to one of the most beautiful highlights of the estate, the
Walled Italian Garden. Here, behind red brick walls and a delicate
wrought-iron gate, is a leafy bower of the kind that must have
attracted the subjects of many a European tale of romance. Although it covers more than two acres, the Italian Garden, by virtue
of ingenious design, has a remarkable sense of intimacy. Some
twenty-five gardeners labor to maintain the estate. The most inten-
sive labor is required for the constant profusion of flowers in the
Italian Garden. In May thousands of bright-colored tulips begin the
yearly show. These are followed by carefully arranged displays of
annuals and biennials — delphinium hybrids, poppies, iris, iberis,
phlox, pansies, sweet William, campanula, foxglove and English
daisies — shown off against the soft red of the brick walls and the
green of espaliered evergreen magnolia, dogwood, yew and arrowwood. At the end of the Gardens' formal path, a baroque water lily
pool, with an outstanding display of water lilies and Egyptian
lotus, is covered by a trellis of grape and wisteria. There is an
aura of serenity here that few American gardens can match. Adjacent to the Italian Garden is the Ghost Walk, a tunnel of hemlock
copied after a similar tunnel of yew at Battle Abbey in Sussex,
England, where Mrs. Phipps lived before she was married. This
leads to a circle of lawn with two bronze peacocks, their tails
sculpted in living yew. Nearby is the Pinetum which, quite

The house and grounds were designed in their present style in 1905-1906 by George Crawley, the famous British architect.

Opposite: The Gardens have a number of trees that, according to the Long Island Horticultural Society, are the largest of their species on Long Island.

properly, has many fine old conifers, including one Korean pine that is among those cited as outstanding by the Long Island Horticultural Society.

In the English Rose Garden a trellis of roses follows the curve of the circular brick path, and hedges of perennial candytuft *(Iberis sempervirens)* enhance the beauty of a superlative collection of hybrid tea roses. In the center of it all is a fine twelve-sided sundial. The path continues and is bordered by the riotous colors of many varieties of primrose. This Primrose Walk leads to one of the most delightful garden areas in all of Old Westbury, the Children's Cottage Garden.

Here behind a tiny white picket fence are the four playhouses that the elder Phipps had built for their four children — three identical log cabins for the three Phipps boys, and, to capture the heart of any little girl, a miniature replica of an English cottage for their only daughter. This tiny thatched cottage with its leaded casements is surrounded by miniature plants: dogwood, hawthorn, small-leaved ivies, rhododendron, azaleas and Dahlborg daisies. This was, as you can imagine, a favorite place for the thirty English children that the Phipps family cared for during World War II.

The family was always a close one, and the spacious gardens as well as Westbury House were designed for comfortable living and entertaining. John S. Phipps carried on the family tradition of generous philanthropy started by his father, Henry Phipps, who is remembered for his generosity in the establishment of the Phipps Conservatory in Pittsburgh, as well as the Henry Phipps Tuberculosis Dispensary in Philadelphia and the Henry Phipps Psychiatric Clinic of Johns Hopkins Hospital in Baltimore.

Not far from the Children's Cottage Garden is the green expanse of the Great South Lawn with its Grand Allée of European linden. From here, the wisteria-covered face of the Georgian brick mansion is seen in a frame of topiary yew. The statuary, such as the Bacchus by the Italian sculptor Varlese, further serves to ornament the scene. It is easy to see why Old Westbury is one of the favorite places for New York fashion photographers to pose their elegant models against the backdrop of garden and mansion.

From the Great Lawn a tunnel leads to a beautiful swimming pool and the large lake with its woodland walk. This is a new addition to the beauty of Old Westbury. Along the edge of the clear lake, and up the slope beside a small brook, the Woodland Walk is bordered with wildflowers growing in their natural habitat under a canopy of towering pine trees. The berries of arrowwood, chokeberry, sweet pepperbush, winterberry and sapphire berry attract the dozens of species that inhabit Old Westbury's bird sanctuary.

At the far end of the lake, the path passes by the bittersweet-covered iron tracery dome and tall graceful columns of the Temple of Love. From here is a lovely view of the Westbury mansion across the length of the lake. As the evening sun sifts through the tall trees and the scent of bittersweet fills the air, there is no doubt that this is a moment from a more peaceful and leisurely time. One almost expects to see some clean-shaven youth, perhaps in a straw skimmer and white ducks, and a girl with the bobbed hair and short dress of the twenties, stroll into the quiet pavilion hand in hand.

Oyster Bay, Long Island, New York

PLANTING FIELDS ARBORETUM

A Gift to the People of New York

Kurume and Glenn Dale hybrid azaleas are planted along this path shaded by dogwood and white pine.

Opposite: Formerly the private estate of the late William Robertson Coe, Planting Fields Arboretum was presented as a gift to the people of the State of New York in 1949.

Even before Planting Fields was donated to the State of New York by the late William Robertson Coe, it was a magnificent estate with fine plantings of rhododendron and stately old trees. Since that time it has been beautifully maintained and thoughtfully improved.

Planting Fields, located at Oyster Bay, Long Island, is near the bay and Long Island Sound and enjoys the moderating effect of the stable temperatures maintained by these two bodies of water. Originally the Matinecock Indians cleared this fertile land for growing corn and other grains, and in their native tongue they called it "planting fields." Indian arrowheads and other relics are still occasionally found here when new land is plowed.

When British settlers took over the land in the early eighteenth century, the English translation of the Indian name for the place remained, and Planting Fields became prosperous farmland. William R. Coe bought the land in 1913.

Coe was a native of Worcestershire, England, and from the first, he decided to grow at Planting Fields those trees and shrubs he loved in England as a boy — especially lindens and beeches, as well as his favorite flowering shrubs, rhododendron and azaleas. After hiring the well-known firm of Olmstead Brothers from Brookline, Massachusetts, to design the original plan for roads, gardens and greenhouses, he set about importing the finest plant specimens he could find. His first purchase, in 1916, was a shipment of *catawbiense* hybrid rhododendron from the Waterer Nursery in England. Many of these original plants, now grown to a great size, still grace the lawns of the estate.

In the early 1920's dozens of sizable specimens of beech trees *(Fagus sylvatica)* in several varieties were planted on the lawns at Planting Fields. Two beautiful silver lindens *(Tilia tomentosa* and *T. petiolaris),* also planted at this time, can still be seen on the lawn just north of the house. A recent publication of the Long Island Horticultural Society lists eighteen trees at Planting Fields as the largest of their kind on the Island. Among them are specimens of golden English elm *(Ulmus procera aurea),* double flowering dogwood *(Cornus florida multibracteata),* incense cedar *(Libocedrus decurrens)* and Atlas cedar *(Cedrus atlantica).* One immense Sargent weeping hemlock measures some fourteen feet tall and forty feet in spread. These fine old trees are now an important part of the Arboretum which has more recently been developed.

As the trees on the estate were being planted, Coe did not neglect his beloved rhododendron and azaleas. For more than forty years he

188

Originally, the Matinecock Indians cleared the fertile lands for growing corn and other grains, calling it "planting fields."

Opposite: The large trees originally planted in the Arboretum give it a deserved quality of age and stability.

continued to seek out new hybrids and the best of the older species. Planting Fields is a virtual fairyland in the spring when the six hundred species of azaleas and rhododendron, and the many magnolias, dogwoods, Japanese cherries and flowering crab apples explode into bloom. Blankets of mountain laurel and Carolina rhododendron cover entire hillsides. Glenn Dale and Kurume hybrids, backed by tall green spires of pine and cedar, line the cool shaded paths with color.

In 1949, Coe arranged in his will and deed to give Planting Fields to the people of the State of New York. Upon his death on March 14, 1955, Planting Fields came under the administrative control of the State University of New York. Of some four hundred acres, 160 were to be permanently preserved and developed as an arboretum. On the remaining land, 200 acres were woodlands and the rest was tillable soil. The seventy-five-room Coe mansion, considered by experts to be one of the finest examples of Elizabethan-style architecture in

Above: This plaque states the Arboretum's guiding principle: "Created for the advancement and enjoyment of horticulture."

Opposite: For over forty years Coe collected and planted outstanding trees and shrubs, particularly rhododendron and azaleas.

Below: An information shelter stands inside the entrance to the Synoptic Garden created by Carl Wedell and Gordon Jones.

the country, was left for the use of the Arboretum. The beautiful detail of work in stone, brick, lead, stained glass and hand-carved wood are outstanding examples of fine craftsmanship.

At the entrance to the gardens from Chicken Valley Road are the famed Carshalton Gates, completed around 1712 by the English craftsman, Thomas Robinson. These gates, enhanced by elegantly sculptured lead statues of Diana, the goddess of the hunt, and the hunter Actaeon, originally marked the entrance to Carshalton Park near London, and were purchased by Coe in 1919.

One reason for Coe giving the estate to the public was the urging of his friend Professor Carl F. Wedell, head of the school of horticulture at Farmingdale Institute. Wedell, who had taken a personal interest in Planting Fields for years, also encouraged Coe to bequeath funds to the Arboretum for its improvement and further development. Under the supervision of Coe's eldest son, William R. Coe, Jr., the Planting Fields Foundation developed the Arboretum into a place where both students of horticulture and the general public could find education and enjoyment.

One of the projects brought before its advisory board, almost as soon as the Arboretum became public, was the idea of a Synoptic Garden, a comprehensive collection of the ornamental shrubs that grow well in the Long Island area. It was not an easy undertaking because of the great number of plant possibilities and the fact that such a project had never been tried. But the advisory board saw its value for students, nurserymen, landscape architects and home-owners, and decided to proceed.

The challenge of designing the Synoptic Garden was given to Carl Wedell after his retirement from Farmingdale Institute. He contin-ues to serve the Arboretum as its executive vice-president and

Above: Inside the Arboretum's one and a half acres of greenhouse, visitors enjoy a fine collection of orchids, anthuriums and hibiscus.

Below: A massive American elm shades the courtyard of the Arboretum's office building, formerly the seventy-five-room Coe mansion.

consulting landscape architect. The unique design that Wedell devised, with the help of Gordon Jones, director of the Arboretum, has proven itself ideal, both for convenience of study as well as esthetic appearance. Jones and Wedell decided, for the sake of easy recognition, to alphabetize the plants by section. With the advice of local horticulturists, more than four hundred shrubs were chosen for the garden. About two-thirds of the five acres of the Synoptic Garden is given over to groupings of three to five or more plants in each species or cultivar. These groupings are arranged in alphabetical order. Thus in section "A-B," are *Abelia, Aesculus, Aronia, Berberis, Buddleia, Buxus.* In section "C," are *Callicarpa, Calluna, Chaenomeles, Cotoneaster.* Each shrub or tree is clearly marked with both its botanical and common name and the area from which it originates. Anyone who wants to see a particular plant can simply look it up in this living dictionary.

The remainder of the garden is devoted to a variety of ground covers, lawns and flowering trees and various garden ornaments. In 1961 an experimental planting of spring bulbs was tried in section "A-B." This was so successful that now, throughout the garden, there are drifts of daffodils, scilla, tulips, anemones, crocus and other bulbs in flower among the shrubbery. The flowers are also labeled for study. As elsewhere in the Arboretum, the large trees originally planted in this area give it the appearance of age and stability.

Other ambitious projects in the Arboretum are under way. In the rhododendron park a large area has been cleared for the inclusion of many *lepidote* (scaly-leaved) species and hybrids. A group of rhododendron species especially suited for growth on Long Island will be selected and arranged in another area for specific study. A conifer trail, lined with many popular species of dwarf conifers as well as the taller conifers, is being laid out.

Inside the Arboretum's one and a half acres of greenhouse, visitors can enjoy the garden's fine collection of orchids, anthuriums, hibiscus and other tropical plants. The Camellia Collection, which Coe began in 1916, is one of the finest in existence. Over 150 *Camellia japonica* and *Camellia reticulata* cultivars bloom from late December through April.

The acres of Planting Fields are enjoyable not only in the spring when the rhododendron and other flowering trees and shrubs blaze into bloom, but also in the expansive green quiet of summer and the flaming brilliance of fall color. The Arboretum's many nature trails are enjoyable in every season.

Almost all of the plants grown in the Arboretum are now labeled and are also included in the herbarium collection. The Arboretum offers an impressive variety and richness of plant materials. Whether one is a student of horticulture or simply a backyard gardener, he will find that Planting Fields is an unforgettable place of quiet beauty and inspiration.

Right: Due to its overhanging tops and somewhat weak branches, the weeping hemlock has a graceful effect.

Below: These weeping Higan cherries are among the first trees to flower at the Arboretum, late in April.

Photos: Courtesy Carroll C. Calkins

196

STERLING FOREST GARDENS

A Garden Setting Which Follows a Dutch Example

Sterling Forest Gardens, near Tuxedo, New York, about an hour north of New York City, is a show-garden unlike any other in the world, and one whose importance extends far beyond that of its plants alone. The Gardens comprise 125 acres of land set in a gentle valley and surrounded by the 22,000 acres of Sterling Forest. Sterling Forest is owned by City Investing Company, and is a varied complex of research and recreational facilities as well as a carefully planned residential community that will eventually include hundreds of families in a carefully planned community. The siting of the houses is strictly controlled and designed to provide as much house-to-house privacy as possible while, at the same time, maintaining the woodland quality of the setting.

The creation of Sterling Forest Gardens as a place of beauty and family entertainment around which a complete community is being developed is an exciting concept which, if successful, could pave the way for others all across the country. It could, perhaps, even start a much-needed movement towards decentralization in America. While the overall plan for Sterling Forest is still a magnificent dream — one that seems well on its way to fruition — it is the Gardens which are a marvelous reality.

The site for Sterling Forest Gardens was chosen by two Dutch landscape architects who were commissioned to create a garden setting similar to the world-famous Keukenhof at Lisse in the heart of the bulb district of Holland. They selected a lovely little valley with a knoll of oak and laurel-covered rock rising gently from the valley floor. Except for this high land, the valley was a virtual swamp. But it was a spectacular setting and the necessary engineering work was undertaken. The swamp was completely dredged and drained to handle the runoff from the hills, and a series of lakes were dug to serve as catch basins. These are connected by an intricate system of dams and underground waterways and it was all so artfully done that the lakes now seem quite natural. The trees reflected in the lakes, the winding paths, green expanses of lawn, great drifts of bulbs in flower and the accents of sculpture give Sterling Forest an overall character much like that of the Keukenhof. But here is the added beauty of the surrounding hills.

Princess Beatrix of The Netherlands planted the first bulb at Sterling Forest in the fall of 1959. A team of Dutch experts then planted more than a million and a half more, which were in full bloom for the opening in the spring of 1960. The Spring Show of bulbs is a major feature of the Gardens and many of the original plantings still continue to flower.

Few are the public gardens where such concentrated effort is made to maintain large areas of bloom from spring to fall.

Opposite: Sculpture accents throughout the Sterling Forest Gardens give it an overall character similar to Keukenhof in Holland.

Gottscho-Schleisner, Inc.

After the first two or three years Sterling Forest began to take on certain American characteristics. A Peacock Train was introduced to make it easier to get around. An All-America Rose Display Garden was established. There is now a Poetry Garden where flowers mentioned by poets through the ages are displayed with appropriate quotations. The Slice of Time is a fascinating display that puts the gardens in their proper chronological perspective. The huge boulder, an important feature of the display, is estimated to be 100 million years old and was transported all the way from Canada by a glacier moving at the rate of a quarter of an inch a year.

Colorful birds were introduced and many of them roam free. Here one can see flamingos, peacocks, Asian demoiselles and African crown-crested cranes in addition to the familiar swans, geese and ducks which the visiting children enjoy feeding. In the Farmyard Theatre trained domestic animals go through their paces in a series of shows each day, and the picnic grounds, tent-covered restaurant and playground are only a few of the attractions to delight the Gardens' guests.

For all its added features and facilities, however, Sterling Forest Gardens is essentially a garden, and as such is one of the most colorful to be seen anywhere. Few are the public gardens where such concentrated effort is made to maintain such large areas of successive bloom from spring to fall. The cool climate and the surrounding hills make the valley a frost pocket, so the season of bloom starts here somewhat later than it does in the average garden in the New York area. This proves to be an advantage for flower lovers, for here one can see a second season of muscari, daffodil, hyacinth and tulips long after they have come and gone in most other gardens.

The Gardens open on the first of May with a spectacular extravaganza of spring gaiety. More than 600,000 flowering spring bulbs are used here. In one area alone some 25,000 tulips are planted in a series of four forty-foot circles of color. Sweeping drifts of narcissus and muscari are naturalized on the hillsides and the hues become brighter as the flowers spread year after year.

There is a unique Tulip Library where 139 of the best varieties available today are beautifully grown and displayed. The Mutation Garden is a living history of the "sports" that have developed naturally to become famous varieties on their own. One such variety is Murillo, which has seventeen sports. Here one finds the original and all its variations together.

Once the pageant of floral color has begun it continues until the curtain is literally rung down in October by the falling of the brilliant foliage on the surrounding hills.

Formal beds are kept full of flowers all season long. Of exceptional beauty is the Grand Tapestry Garden, a vast carpet of blue and yellow pansies, flower urns and fountains set off by colored gravel. The design, based on Aubusson and Millesfleurs tapestries, is stunning in its conception. The Garden's spring show is supplemented by the native amelanchier, crab apple, azalea (*R. nudiflorum*), mountain laurel and dogwood flowers.

Opposite: The first spring blooms offer a startling contrast with the stark baldness of the surrounding trees.

Above: Princess Beatrix of The Netherlands planted the first bulb at Sterling Forest in the fall of 1959.

Below: A series of lakes which serve as catch basins are connected by an intricate system of dams and waterways.

Photos: Gottscho-Schleisner, Inc.

200

In the summer annuals such as marigolds and ageratum are used in the Tapestry Garden. *Begonia semperflorens* fill the various planting beds with dazzling hues. In shady places are impatiens, coleus, browallia and tradescantia. In the sun the petunias, geraniums, snapdragons, cannas, lantana, sunflowers and zinnias by the thousands display their brilliance. Many flowering shrubs and small trees are used all through the garden to enhance the summer color, and, of course, this is the season when the Rose Garden is at its best.

The fall is chrysanthemum time. Some 17,000 of these dependable beauties are grown in the nursery here and planted in the beds as needed to replace the summer annuals before they fade — not after, but before. The rich colors of the chrysanthemums combine with the brilliant foliage of the deciduous trees on the surrounding hills to close the season with a blaze of glory in October.

Everything, however, is not on such a spectacular scale. There is a lovely display of popular annual and perennial flowers planted in beds of manageable size so gardeners can visualize how they would look in their own backyards.

The obvious interest in take-home ideas spurred the development of the Home Garden of Ideas. This is a unique demonstration garden in which there are some thirty specific ideas for home landscaping designs and plantings. There are ideas for paving, fencing and edging. There is a redwood deck, trellis for vines, herb garden, fountain, planter benches and a lath umbrella for hanging plants. Outstanding small trees, shrubs, ground covers and container plants are shown. While the demonstration garden is a carefully integrated whole, it is actually a series of separate ideas. Its purpose is to suggest specific ideas that can be adapted to one's own garden. The garden is sponsored by the Chemical Bank and was created by the editors of *Home Garden Magazine* working with the noted landscape architect, Armand Benedek.

Sterling Forest Gardens is not like any other and could well be called a "Corporate Estate." It is essentially the product of banking and real estate interests whose larger goal is the development of Sterling Forest. Fortunately, however, the design was under the control of one or two strong-minded individuals and thus the Gardens have a common bond with the nation's great estate gardens. It is perhaps through this combination of corporate finance, individual enthusiasm and visitors who pay their way that horticultural displays on a grand scale may still be established and maintained in this country.

Opposite above: On the banks of International Lake, tulips are used both in mass plantings and in a giant necklace complete with pendants.

Opposite below: In the unique Tulip Library, backyard gardeners may inspect 139 of the best varieties available today.

Courtesy Carroll C. Calkins

Above: More than 25,000 tulips are planted in four forty-foot circles in the Flower Circle Plaza.

Below: While the overall plan for Sterling Forest is still a magnificent dream, the Gardens are a marvelous reality.

Gottscho-Schleisner, Inc.

Newport, Rhode Island

THE ELMS

From Newport's Gilded Age

The historic city of Newport, Rhode Island, some thirty miles from Providence at the entrance to Narragansett Bay, has long been known as an exclusive summer enclave for the wealthy. Season after season huge, opulent mansions such as The Breakers, Marble House, Miramar and The Elms have seen entertainments unparalleled in their magnificence.

Newport life at the turn of the century was a perpetual gala sailing in the bay, swimming, garden parties, lawn parties, automobile races, horseback riding and always a Saturday evening ball. It is said that during the Newport summer season, if there was no other ball or large party scheduled for Saturday evening, the Berwinds at The Elms were always ready to provide the occasion.

Edward Julius Berwind was a self-made man, one of those *nouveaux riches* who, according to tradition, was unacceptable to Newport society. The Berwinds, however, managed to breach the tradition. The son of a German emigrant, a cabinetmaker who worked in a piano factory, Edward Berwind was born in Philadelphia in 1848. Some years later, in 1865, President Lincoln named the enterprising young man to the United States Naval Academy. He graduated, but gave up his commission in 1875 to join his three brothers and Judge Allison White in founding the Berwind, White Company, later to be known as the Berwind-White Coal Mining Company. By 1876 he was in charge of the company's headquarters in New York.

The company grew rapidly, and soon was the principal coal supplier of our country's merchant marine. From tens of thousands of acres of coal land in West Virginia, Pennsylvania and Kentucky, the company fulfilled its large contracts with France and Italy, as well as with the United States Navy. By the time The Elms was built in 1901, the company was the largest owner of coal mining property in the United States.

In 1887 Edward J. Berwind married Miss Herminie Torrey, a young English woman, and soon after purchased a Newport home called The Elms, a smaller predecessor of The Elms we know today. By 1894 the couple was living in an Italian palace on New York's Fifth Avenue, and five years later he decided to replace the Newport cottage with something larger.

After the present version of The Elms was commissioned, Mr. and Mrs. Berwind traveled to Europe, returning to Newport in the summer of 1901 to a housewarming party which was one of the major events of the season. Along the main terrace, pink, blue and

Near the Sunken Garden is a copy of Taddeo Landini's Turtle Fountain. Four boys hold small turtles on the rim of the basin.

Opposite: Designed by the Philadelphia architect Horace Trumbauer, The Elms is a rather severe looking stone mansion in the French classical style.

Courtesy Preservation Society of Newport County

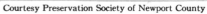

white hydrangeas circled pots of palms, orchids and other exotic plants. Bright lights illuminated the huge palm tree in the Park (outlined with white flowers) and the orange grove on the South Terrace. The house was colorfully festooned with a profusion of American Beauty roses from the floor to the ceiling. Two orchestras alternated in the gigantic ballroom, while outside in the Park, the Newport Band attempted to outdo the chattering of dozens of tame monkeys rented for the evening and let loose on the lawn.

The Elms, a rather severe looking stone mansion in the French classical style, was designed by a Philadelphia architect, Horace Trumbauer. Though Trumbauer is little remembered today, at the time he was well known for planning several private homes such as the Stotesbury mansion at Chestnut Hill, Pennsylvania, and the James Buchanan Duke home in New York, as well as such public architectural projects as the campus of Duke University at Durham, North Carolina, and the Philadelphia Museum of Art.

Modeled after the early eighteenth-century Château d'Argenson at Asnières, France, The Elms is an outstanding example of both architectural and landscape design. The main pavilion centered in the east facade is elaborately decorated, but the mansion achieves distinction primarily through its classic proportions. The west or garden facade is embellished by four life-size baroque sculptural groupings at the ends of the parapet and its junctions with the central pavilion. Behind this parapet is hidden the third-story servants' quarters with sixteen large rooms and three baths. These hidden rooms, along with the basement kitchen and the heating plant in a sub-basement, made it possible for The Elms to be maintained as if by magic. No work areas were visible from the main part of the house.

The garden facade is an impressive sight. It faces two terraces, a broad expanse of lawn enhanced with trees and the formal gardens lying beyond. Although the gardens were laid out by Charles H.

Above: The magnificent view from the Terrace includes one of the two marble gazebos which mark the entrance to the Sunken Garden.

Opposite: The front of the mansion is planted with bright rhododendron that stand out clearly against the colorless stone.

Above: The Sunken Garden contains lush plantings of begonias edged with boxwood hedges. At the center is an Italian wellhead.

Left: Along an inviting pathway bordered with ivy there is a thick hedge with niches, each displaying a marble bust on a pedestal.

Miller and Ernest W. Bowditch, they reflect the architectural presence of Horace Trumbauer. They are fully integrated with the overall design of the estate and, with their teahouses and Sunken Garden, they show as much of the architect's craft as that of the landscape designer. Another important influence on the development of the gardens was Bruce Butterton, gardener at The Elms for many years, who selected and placed the plants.

A survey of the grounds takes us first to the gates of the estate on Bellevue Avenue. From here we can view the mansion's east facade through a gate of finely executed wrought iron, topped by a rampant lion and flanked by posts surmounted with garlanded urns. Between the gates and the graveled drive is a grove of trees, skillfully shaped and tended. Here specimens of copper beech *(Fagus sylvatica purpurea)*, Norway maple *(Acer platanoides)*, katsura tree *(Cercidiphyllum japonicum sinense)*, linden, and even the unusually unkempt maidenhair tree *(Ginkgo biloba)* are carefully trimmed and tailored to shape.

On the far side of the drive, masses of brilliant rhododendron and a ground cover of pachysandra lead to the wall of the Main Terrace traced with the green leaves and tiny blue flowers of plumbago. A walk to the south and west leads past American arborvitae and Pfitzer junipers *(Juniperus chinensis pfitzeriana)* to a magnificent old beech tree and a marble bench.

The Terrace, which can be entered only from the ends or from the mansion, extends along the garden facade. On the upper level of the Terrace are imposing pieces of sculpture, including a bronze *Lion and Crocodile*, dated 1889 and signed "Allard" (a French decorating firm), and a bronze group, *The Madness of Athamas*, created in 1880 by Pio Fede (1816-1892). Beside the door which opens from the ballroom in the central pavilion to the Terrace are two sculptural groups, Apollo and Aphrodite. Above the door is a huge carved stone mask of Neptune that looks out on the Terrace and the fine old maples, beeches, lindens and oaks that stand nobly on the lawn or Park. A path leads through the lawn to a bronze fountain surrounded by sea nymphs, satyrs, sea horses and the scene of Hercules grappling with the Hydra.

An inviting pathway bordered with ivy leads to the Sunken Garden. Along the path there is a thick hedge with small niches, each displaying a marble bust on a tall pedestal. And at the end of the path on a small terrace is a reproduction of the Turtle Fountain *(Fontana delle Tartarugho,* Rome, circa 1550-1596) by Taddeo Landini. Two marble teahouses or gazebos, covered with wisteria, mark the entrance to the Sunken Garden which is of formal design and filled with a lush planting of pink begonias edged with boxwood hedges. At the center is an Italian wellhead circled by a frieze of dancing cherubs and a goat. A path on the south side of the lawn leads back to the villa.

After Mrs. Berwind's death in 1922, Mr. Berwind's sister Julia became hostess at The Elms. She continued to summer there regularly, even after the passing of her brother, until she died in

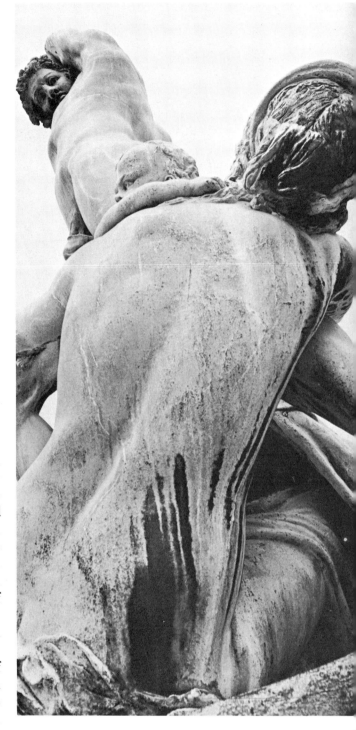

The Madness of Athamas, a bronze group by Pio Fede, shows the crazed son of Aeolus slaying his son Learchus.

In addition to its principal subject, this complex bronze fountain of Hercules killing the Hydra has many elements: sea nymphs, sea horses and carousing satyrs.

Opposite: On the Terrace is a bronze *Lion and Crocodile* signed "Allard" and dated 1889. Allard et Fils was one of two Parisian decorating firms contracted by Trumbauer.

1961 at the age of ninety-one. The Berwind heirs decided to sell the estate to a syndicate that planned to demolish the old mansion and subdivide the property. However, the Preservation Society of Newport County raised sufficient funds from private contributions to buy the estate for the purpose of turning it into a museum and cultural center.

The list of donors and lenders to The Elms reads like a page from the Social Register — Mr. and Mrs. John Alden Carpenter, Mr. and Mrs. John R. Drexel III, Miss Doris Duke, Mr. Henry F. du Pont, Mrs. Harvey S. Firestone, Jr., Mrs. John Jay Ide and many others. All of these people, many of whom have large estates of their own, recognized the historical importance of this Newport landmark and realized that gardens of this scale may never again be possible.

Today The Elms is a showcase. Special exhibits are held regularly in its elegant rooms. And, of course, the architecture and some of the furnishings, intact as they were in the early 1900's, are a nostalgic reminder of America's Golden Age.

Stockbridge, Massachusetts

NAUMKEAG

On the Slopes of the Berkshires

The charm of Naumkeag lies not only in its present beauty, but in the *gradual* change it has seen throughout almost a century. The massive old house, with its sloping lawns and flower gardens, was the summer home of New York lawyer Joseph Choate in Stockbridge, Massachusetts, then called "the inland Newport." The house stands today, as it did in the 1890's, overlooking the Berkshire Hills, a symbol of the Golden Age in this part of America.

The Hon. Joseph Hodges Choate, a modest, charming Harvard graduate born in Salem, Massachusetts, became one of the most respected lawyers in the country. His prosecution of the Boss Tweed ring in New York City, and the Standard Oil antitrust cases brought him national eminence and in 1899 he was named Ambassador to Great Britain. For all his growing fame, Choate was known to his Stockbridge neighbors as a witty and unpretentious man, little concerned with elegant dress, who always had time to stop for a chat.

The Choates were a close knit and happy family that, for years, had picnicked and summered in Stockbridge. But it was not until 1884 that Choate convinced David Dudley Field, his opponent in the Boss Tweed affair, to sell his "lower forty" on the west side of Prospect Hill. The Choate family decided to call their new summer home Naumkeag, which was the Indian name for Salem and meant "Haven of Peace." It was, however, conceived in sadness because the Choates' eldest son Ruluff, home from Harvard, suddenly became ill and died.

Naumkeag was located in the steep hills about three-quarters of a mile from the center of Stockbridge. As their architects, the family chose the famous New York firm of McKim, Mead and White who had designed the Rhode Island State House, the Boston Library, Madison Square Garden and Pennsylvania Station.

By Stockbridge standards the twenty-six-room, Norman-style mansion, complete with gables and turrets, was a modest one. This was the center of New England's aristocracy and included some of the largest houses ever built in America: Italian and Gothic castles, an exact replica of the Petit Trianon, a Louis XIV château, Tudor and Stuart mansions and a Queen Anne's manorial palace. As a visitor to Stockbridge, the poet Matthew Arnold regarded the enormous houses through his lifted monocle and observed that they were, "pretty and coquettish, not beautiful."

Summers in Stockbridge were a gay social whirl. There were soirées, theater and lawn parties, bicycling and horseback riding

A bronze boy-and-stork statue by Frederick MacMonnies decorates the corner of the flagstone-paved Afternoon Garden.

Opposite: Near the tile-roofed Chinese Temple in the Chinese Garden at Naumkeag, a marble table and marble-cushioned stools suggest a recently completed game of mah-jongg.

through the hills, boating on the Housatonic, cricket and croquet matches and tennis tournaments. The season ended each year with a costumed street dance, a bonfire and a mad torchlight parade through Ice Glen.

The Choate family was popular with both the social set and the other people of the town. Choate's two daughters began to furnish the house with the tables, chairs, lamps and other pieces that have since become valuable antiques. Mr. Choate, who was brought up to work hard in Salem, enjoyed the rigors of farm life. His talented wife gave art lessons to her neighbors, and Joseph Choate, Jr., introduced the game of golf to the Berkshires. He came home from Canada one year with three curious-looking sticks with which he knocked a ball into sunken tomato cans. Three years later he went on to set record-breaking scores at the National Golf Championship.

The gardens of Naumkeag, designed by Nathaniel F. Barrett, were a challenging project, complicated by steep hillsides and narrow valleys. The main formal gardens north of the house were divided by a wide entrance drive. The Upper Garden, on a steep hillside, was planted with beds of herbaceous flowers in ornate shield patterns outlined by graveled paths. The Lower Garden, terraced almost flat, was planted with oblong beds of annuals. At the center of this garden was a circular fountain and a statue of a boy and stork by a then little-known sculptor, Frederick Mac-Monnies (1863-1937). A graceful pergola overlooked the house and valley below. Evergreen hedges of spruce surrounded the Upper Garden and hemlocks enclosed the lower.

Opposite: Naumkeag, an Indian name meaning "Haven of Peace," is located in sharp hills three-quarters of a mile from Stockbridge.

Below: The Afternoon Garden contains four small fountains surrounding a shallow black-mirror pool designed by Claude Lorraine.

Paul E. Genereux

Photos: Paul E. Genereux

Above: The Blue Steps, designed by Fletcher Steele, are Dantesque stairways, each with its ramp and roofed basin set into the hillside.

Below: The Moon Gate is a curious feature of the Chinese Garden, which was created to unify the stone Buddhas, lions, dogs and figures Miss Choate obtained in the Orient in 1935.

To the west of the mansion, two broad terraced lawns sloped sharply downward, the delight of visiting children who would roll down them. Below this a hillside covered with lilacs led to the greenhouse, orchards and a cutting garden.

The South Lawn was a steep hillside which fell toward an ancient great white oak, the largest tree on the estate. On the flat lawn beyond was the tennis court, and beyond this a woods of young trees planted after the estate was purchased. Mrs. Choate traveled twice to Europe during the 1890's and was much taken with the tree lined walks she saw there, particularly the famous *"Unter der Linden"* of Germany. On her return she planted the double row of linden trees *(Tilia cordata)* on the South Lawn.

In the spring of 1917, not long after he was the dinner host at his New York home for a glittering company including the renowned British Foreign Secretary, Arthur James Balfour, the French philosopher Henri Bergson and Nicholas Murray Butler, President of Columbia University, the indomitable, eighty-five-year-old Joseph Hodges Choate fell ill and died. He lived a full life and once told the novelist Theodore Dreiser that the man who earns success and the surroundings of luxury is "really the one whose life has been a constant refutation of the need of these things. . . . His enjoyment has been in working."

Choate's daughter Mabel chose to remain at Naumkeag with her mother where, following her own interest in gardening, she gradually remodeled the estate. It was she who moved and transformed the old Stockbridge Casino into the present Berkshire Theatre and Art Gallery.

At a meeting of the Lenox Garden Club in the late 1920's someone suggested to Fletcher Steele, a distinguished landscape architect from Boston, that he should see the gardens at Naumkeag. On his first encounter with Mabel Choate he suggested to her that nothing could be done with the place until some change was made in the back entrance — a drive surrounded by a dilapidated lattice fence and too narrow for anything but a horse and buggy.

The two began at once to make plans. Miss Choate had found to her dismay that there was no cool shady place to sit comfortably outdoors in the afternoon. She decided to have an Afternoon Garden. The south entrance was leveled and made into a patio with four small fountains surrounding a shallow black-mirror pool designed by Claude Lorraine. The MacMonnies statue was brought from the front of the house and placed in the corner of the garden. Fletcher Steele obtained some oak pilings that were dredged from a seventy-five-year stay at the bottom of Boston Harbor and had them carved and colored to resemble Venetian pillars. They were placed around the garden under a shady canopy of elms and twined with vines of clematis. Tables of yellow tile, pink Roman thrones, beautiful benches of wrought iron and sunken beds of lilies and lobelias made this an idyllic outdoor room for a peaceful afternoon.

The success of the Afternoon Garden marked the beginning of a friendship between Steele and Miss Choate that was to flourish for more than thirty years. Steele admired the original Nathaniel Barrett design. He did not want to change it, but improvements were needed to unify the gardens and to make the grounds more manageable. The flower gardens to the north of the house required the work of several gardeners. The West Lawn, with its steep, grassy hillside, was all but impossible to mow. Under Fletcher Steele's direction the front gardens were made into the Green Gardens, the top slope planted with broad-leafed evergreens, and the lower one with dwarf pines. Flowers were concentrated in the area of the Cutting Garden. The terraces of the West Lawn were converted into a rock garden of flat, irregular stones and three terraces of richly blooming tree peonies.

Mabel Choate entered into the project with the excitement that only a born gardener can know. One day, while walking down the highway near Naumkeag, she noticed a dump truck full of dirt go by, and then another. She stopped one of the trucks to ask where it was going. To the village dump, said the driver; a neighbor was building an addition to her house and this dirt had to be removed. She was informed that she could have it for fifty cents a load. Miss Choate called Fletcher Steele in Boston and he said to buy all she could and have it dumped on the South Lawn.

The South Lawn was consequently converted into a graded terrace, gently falling from the Afternoon Garden to the Linden Walk, with a wide border of myrtle. The steep bank below is covered with ivy and clematis, and beyond is a great oak tree and level lawn. Edging the curve of the terrace is a slim, graceful line of pollarded larch trees.

From the Afternoon Garden to the Cutting Garden through a grove of lilacs, the way was steep and often slippery. Finally Miss

Above: Lining the Afternoon Garden on the south side of the gabled Norman-style mansion are oak pilings resembling Venetian pillars.

Below: Ribbon-like pathways of marble chips trace a whimsical design in the hillside Rose Garden of floribundas.

Paul E. Genereux

215

Nathaniel F. Barrett, designer of the gardens at Naumkeag, was faced with the challenge of adapting the steep Berkshire hillsides.

Choate asked Fletcher Steele if he would design some steps for this slope. Little did she expect the magnificent plan he presented for the Blue Steps, one of the most attractive aspects of the garden. They descend the bank from the Afternoon Garden, divide into two tiers at the top and circle back on themselves to form a ramp down which water flows from the black-mirror basin. The design is repeated three times, each set of steps with its ramp and roofed basin. The steps of cement were painted blue to correspond with the posts in the Afternoon Garden. The banks on each side were planted with a thick stand of white birches.

After her mother's death in 1929, Mabel Choate traveled a great deal. In 1935 she went to Tokyo with other members of the Garden Club of America to attend their annual meeting. The beauty of the Orient so delighted her that she and a friend decided to travel on to Peking where they rented a house for a month. The Chinese stonework and carvings fascinated Miss Choate. She bought many fine pieces and had them crated and shipped home. Upon her return, there they were, standing about in the yard and not a single piece broken.

One day, not long after, Ralph Adams Cram, a famous architect of the day, accompanied Fletcher Steele to Naumkeag. He unhesitatingly took Miss Choate to task for leaving the precious stone figures sitting on the lawn directly exposed to all weather, and said she must build a proper shelter for them. Steele agreed, and soon the three had decided on the perfect site for the Chinese House — on a terrace against a wall above the Herbaceous Garden.

The Chinese House was soon built, circled by a grove of ginkgo trees and a mossy, rock-filled Chinese Garden with a marble table and stools. Water trickles softly through marble channels among the garden rocks. Around this garden is a red brick wall roofed with tiles, resembling the one that surrounds the Forbidden City in Peking. There is even a twisting Devil Screen entrance to keep the devils away. On the steps to the Chinese House, approached by the Spirit Walk, is a flat stone carved with the Imperial Dragon over which the Emperor alone was permitted to be carried in his sedan chair. It was thought that this stone would protect him from evil spirits. Inside the Chinese "temple" are the stone Buddhas, lions and other treasures that Miss Choate collected in her travels.

One piece, the ancient Sacred Rock on its Ming pedestal, from the Summer Palace at Peking, was given a special place in a small pagoda on the South Lawn, near the entrance to the Linden Walk. Around this ironwork pagoda with its painted red roof is a fan of red Japanese maples. The view from here looks back across the verdant lawn toward the mansion. Nearby is the last addition that Miss Choate made to her beloved grounds — a Rose Garden of floribundas outlined with curving marble paths.

Miss Choate, who died in 1958, bequeathed Naumkeag to The Trustees of Reservations, a charitable corporation which preserves for the public, places of natural beauty and historical interest in Massachusetts. Over the years the gardens have softened and changed, but change at Naumkeag has meant beauty, and the spot remains a lovely tribute to a dedicated gardener and great landscape designer from an era of Victorian elegance.

Above: Looking from the Chinese Temple, one sees the rolling Berkshire Hills in the background and the twisting Devil Screen entrance designed to thwart the devil.

Left: At the entrance to the Linden Walk, a red-roofed Chinese Pagoda enshrines on a Ming pedestal the ancient Sacred Rock brought by Miss Choate from the Peking summer palace.

217

STONE CHIMNEY GARDEN

Among Vermont's Historic Hills

The magic of Stone Chimney Garden springs equally from its rocky, fertile soil and from its heritage of history and tradition, recalling New England as it was settled by the rugged pioneers. Stone Chimney is a woodland garden near Reading, Vermont. In 1942 the owners, Mr. and Mrs. Hollis Newton, were drawn back to the country their ancestors settled. They bought an old farmhouse built in 1812 by Jonathan Shedd in a clearing surrounded by wooded hills. All that was left of the once prosperous farm was a barn, two outbuildings and some fine old apple trees.

While Hollis Newton put his carpentry skill to work at restoring the old buildings, his wife, Elizabeth, labored to rebuild the stone-wall fences she loves. And, here, with a magnificent view of Mt. Ascutney, framed by the distant hills, she planted the Stone Chimney Garden — an acre of flowers — watered by a spring in the mountains.

The landmarks around Stone Chimney Garden stand as a living legend of this historic land. One mile to the south is Bailey's Mills. The old woolen mill, built by Levi Bailey, has long since disappeared, but the brick building that was the Bailey's home and the local post office has had good care and may soon become an inn. It has a ballroom and a secret room that was probably used as a stop on the Underground Railroad. About a mile through the woods to the north of the Garden, stands the stone chimney for which the place was named — a famous landmark in the area. Though the name of the family who first lived here is lost to history, nature has made it a memorable place. An old road, now a fern-lined walk through the woods, leads to the large chimney, built entirely without mortar, that provided the draft for two fireplaces and an oven. Near the chimney stands a giant white birch tree. As one of the largest and oldest trees of its kind in existence it is protected by the Reading Historical Society.

The Stone Chimney Garden, in the midst of the lovely green hills of Vermont, has an unspoiled setting of unsurpassed charm. Its blooming season begins with the parting of the snows in April and the first pink and white bells of heather *(Erica carnea),* patches of arbutus, Juliana primroses, spring saxifrage, native hepaticas and pale green fern croziers. But this is only a prelude to the grand show of hundreds of primulas and many other plants that follows.

Primulas and heather are specialties of Stone Chimney Garden. In the Primrose or Shady Garden, a combination of native ferns, wild-flowers, bulb flowers, spring flowering perennials and dozens of varieties of primroses are set in raised beds edged with stone and

It is not uncommon to see azaleas with a second color, often in the form of dots. Curiously, these markings usually appear only on one or two of the uppermost petals.

Opposite: A mile through the woods to the north of Stone Chimney stands the structure which gave the Garden its name. The giant birch nearby is one of the largest of its kind.

Tucked into the rock borders among rare ferns and wildflowers is a collection of rock garden favorites and delicate Alpine plants.

surrounded by dirt paths in intricate patterns among the flowers. There are many stone walls, so typical of New England, for background and shade for low-growing plants. Moss and lichen-covered rock, old stumps and moss-covered logs provide a lovely natural setting for enchanting beds of flowers.

By the first of May the Shady Garden is bright with color. The earliest primroses to bloom are denticulatas, the Asiatic primroses with attractive spherical heads of blue flowers. Soon to follow are the gay Julianas, the auriculas with their fragrant yellow flowers and then the tall candelabra primroses. The polyanthas at Stone Chimney are Barnhaven originals in white, yellow, sunset, spice, velvety wine reds, blue, pink and silver. Along with this primrose spectacular there are tulips, fritillary (both the *F. imperialis* and *F. pudicia)*, narcissus and hundreds of wildflowers. Drifts of pink and white hepaticas, trilliums, jack-in-the-pulpits, yellow and blue violets, gentians, and partridge berry brighten the shady woodland.

The primrose season lasts from May until June when the Shady Garden cools from its blaze of color to become a green glade of rare ferns and wildflowers. Dappled by sun and shadow are the delicate green fronds of maidenhair fern, beech fern, oak fern, narrow-leaved spleenwort, lady fern and a variety of others. Tucked into the rock borders and among the other flowers is a collection of rock garden favorites and delicate Alpine plants, some of which are quite rare.

The Perennial Garden is of formal design. In the center is a small pool and a low rock wall and shrubs as a background. Dwarf boxwood *(Buxus microphylla koreana)* is perfectly hardy here at Stone Chimney as are the specimens of *Buxus sempervirens* planted around the pool. In the perennial beds, peonies, iris, salmon-pink Oriental poppies, phlox, lavender, pink dianthus, chrysanthemums and a wealth of other colorful favorites create a display that lasts all through the flowering season.

By July, the Heather Garden, one of the highlights of Stone Chimney, is bright with mid-summer color. Most people think of heather only as the purple tapestry flung out over the British moors. But there is a wide variety of heaths and heathers in many colors and forms affording interest and beauty from early spring to late fall. The slender spikes of the common heather of the moors, *Calluna vulgaris,* bloom through August and September while the foliage heathers are at their best in October. *Erica carnea,* a shrubby, south European species, blooms in spring — as the snow is melting here. Its bell-like blossoms vary from white to purple and bright pink. Altogether more than twenty-five varieties of ericas grow in the Heather Garden — including *E. cinerea* or bell heather and cross-leaved heather *(E. tetralix)* among them.

Around the Garden are shrubs and flowering trees to contrast with the low-growing heather. Azaleas and native mountain laurel lend their pink and white bloom to the spring. Dwarf evergreens, juniper, pale yellow cytisus, the pendulous white flowers of enkianthus, and the andromeda bring considerable variety to the lovely Heather Garden.

Right: The massive stone chimney that once provided the draft for two fireplaces and an oven overlooks the lovely hills of Vermont.

Below: One feature of the Garden is the typical New England stone wall, used for background and shade for low-growing plants.

In the beginning Mrs. Newton gave away cuttings and garden flowers to her visitors, but now that so many people come here this is no longer possible. Some of the varieties are for sale, however, although no wildflowers or ferns are available. They are strictly for the pleasure of viewing in the wild and for the purpose of conservation and study.

Like all true gardeners, Elizabeth Newton enjoys sharing her knowledge and love for gardening with others. As chairman of the Northeast Wild Flower Preservation Society and as host chairman for the Federated Garden Clubs of Vermont, she travels and lectures frequently on her favorite subject. Though Stone Chimney Garden is open throughout the spring and summer months, Mrs. Newton prefers that visitors coming from long distances make advance appointments, since she runs the lovely, woodland garden by herself and is away on tour from time to time.

Stone Chimney Garden evokes a still beautiful and unspoiled New England. Looking over the shady plots of wildflowers, of primroses and heather, at the timeless stone walls, the old farm house and the large pond nearby, mirroring the quiet background of mountains and woods, one can only hope that other such places will remain untrammeled in the face of a fast-moving civilization. If this is to happen, it will be the gardeners, with their respect for nature's forces, who will lead the way.

Opposite: Hundreds of wildflowers and dozens of varieties of primroses are set in the Shady Garden in raised beds edged with stone.

Above: Colorful narcissus offset the delicate green fronds of maidenhair fern, beech fern, oak fern and a variety of others.

Below: The calceolaria originated principally in South and Central America. It is unusual to see them except at large flower shows.

Mansfield, Ohio

KINGWOOD CENTER

A Garden and a Meeting Place

Kingwood Center in Mansfield, Ohio, the forty-seven-acre estate of the late Charles Kelley King, bears the stamp of Midwestern hominess and hospitality that is sometimes lacking in the larger Eastern gardens. The gardening here centers around the flowers that can easily be cultivated by the amateur, and the Center itself is a busy meeting place for local garden enthusiasts and a cultural center for the Mansfield area.

Before visiting the Center's formal gardens and flower beds, a walk through the nature trails and bird sanctuary provides a refreshing insight into the character of this part of the country when it was first settled more than a century ago. Tall old hardwoods (maples, oaks, elms and walnuts) and giant conifers, stand high above the mossy forest floor. In spring there are wildflowers scattered through the shady woods. The jack-in-the-pulpits, trilliums, violets, sweet Williams, and other small heralds of spring such as mushrooms, ferns and delicate, waxy Indian pipes rise through the leaves as they have done for centuries.

The Center's wildlife conservation program was started by Lloyd S. Barr, a Mansfield naturalist, well known for his knowledge of Ohio plants and animals. After he retired from business Mr. Barr worked part time at Kingwood, laying out the nature trails with all varieties of Ohio plant life, and developing a population of wild birds and animals. For this wildlife conservation project he raised pheasants, quail, chukars, ducks and other birds to help increase their number in Kingwood's large bird sanctuary.

By now many of the birds are so tame that they happily feed on bread and grain given them by the visitors, and they offer an intimate view of bird life seldom seen even by hunters. The sanctuary is a favorite haunt of local bird watchers since it attracts a variety of uncommon birds, including the rare pileated woodpecker. Several caged birds, a pair of shy red foxes, a raccoon named Fritzy and an opossum add to the wildlife collection and are used by the staff naturalist for lecture demonstrations.

Kingwood Hall, a stately three-story French Provincial mansion, stands in the center of well-manicured lawns, formal gardens and large shade trees. From 1926 until his death in 1952, this was the home of Charles Kelley King, an Ohio businessman who lived his own Horatio Alger story. When King was but two months away from getting his degree in electrical engineering at Johns Hopkins University, his father died at their home in Maine, leaving young Charles to support his mother and three younger sisters. Moving to

In Kingwood's Rose Garden, intriguing and promising varieties, many as yet unnamed, give a hint of what future rose lovers will grow.

Opposite: One of the features of the Terrace Garden at Kingwood Center is a marble statue, *The Lady of the Gaillardias*.

225

Flowers in the Round Garden are changed twice a year to provide a continual display of floral beauty.

Ohio, the young man involved himself with producing brass fittings for the nation's electric railroads, and from that humble start he rose to the positions of president and chairman of the board of the Ohio Brass Company.

From an early age King showed a lively interest in horticulture. The Kingwood estate, from its very beginning, was intended to become a place for public enjoyment. The childless King loved children and often invited both old and young to join skating parties on the Kingwood pond or use his tennis court and swimming pool during the summer. Each Christmas he sponsored a dance at Kingwood Hall for his two nephews and their young friends.

In 1937-1938, at King's request, the National Recreation Association of New York City conducted an extensive study of the Mansfield area. The program followed now at Kingwood Center is largely based on that study. When King died in 1952, a large portion of his estate was set aside for the purpose of establishing and maintaining this center of gardening, nature study, and cultural activity. Kingwood Center was opened to the public in 1953.

In Kingwood Hall, also open to public use, local nature enthusiasts hold regular meetings. A variety of organizations, such as the Mansfield Men's Garden Club, Kingwood Rose Society, Central Ohio Iris Society and the Ohio Lily Society, sponsor a number of flower shows each year which serve to sharpen the skills of practiced gardeners and to interest others in the art of growing flowers. The members of these organizations take a family interest in the functions of Kingwood Center. In the summer local bands and orchestras play concerts on the lawn of Kingwood Hall. Local theatre guilds, art clubs, stamp and coin collectors, and other groups present a series of displays and performances. Lecturers from various fields of horticulture and botany are invited to speak on a variety of subjects, and the garden's own naturalists and horticulturists are available for lectures and programs. In addition to these regular services, the Center's employees answer scores of questions by mail or telephone for uncertain or frustrated home gardeners.

The Kingwood greenhouses do not specialize in rare or exotic plants as do many conventional greenhouses. The interest here is in plants that can be grown indoors by the amateur gardener. Since all parts of the greenhouses are open to the public, visitors can observe each variety, from cutting or seedling to its full growth. In summer or winter the temperature-controlled greenhouses are comfortable to visit and alive with sparkling floral beauty. It is not a rare occurrence for the visitor who notices some experimental plant not yet on the market to be given a cutting for his own garden.

Another popular section of Kingwood Center is the big, quiet library in Kingwood Hall. Here books on every subject, from gemmology to gardening, and from wild animals to cooking with wildflowers, is available to whet the appetite and to encourage study by gardeners and nature lovers. The library originated in the purchase of many volumes from the century-old collection of James Vick, pioneer seedsman and plantsman of Rochester, New York. Since then dozens of volumes have been added to the collection each year. Four hundred nursery and seed catalogues are available for the delectation of flower shoppers.

The acres of gardens at Kingwood Center are a favorite place for club tours, for Scout and school nature walks, for Mansfield citizens who wish to spend a pleasant afternoon, and for visitors from all over the country. One of Kingwood's stated goals — and one it accomplishes admirably — is to encourage American gardening as an art form.

Because the blooming season is shorter here in central Ohio than in many parts of the country, the emphasis is on displaying as much floral beauty as possible between late March and mid-November. In the spring the first sign of life here, as in many northern gardens, is the show of Dutch crocus. By mid-April the woods at Kingwood Center come alive with thousands of naturalized narcissus. Trumpet, large and small, triandus, cyclamineus, tazetta, jonquilla, and poeticus all grow in gold and yellow sunbursts against the green, dark, barely wakened woods. From now until late fall the gardens are an everchanging kaleidoscope of color.

Then comes the spectacular show of tulips. In large, free-form beds cut out of the rolling green lawn, in the sunken garden, in the terrace gardens, and in formal gardens throughout the estate, 70,000 tulips of every color and variety bloom almost simultaneously. Then, when their petals fade and fall, they are spaded up and removed to make room for the flowers to follow.

Many of the flowers here are grown in test plots for the various floral societies. In Kingwood's Rose Garden, promising varieties as

Tall old hardwoods such as maples, oaks, elms and walnuts, and giant conifers date from a century ago, when the land was settled.

Kingwood is a favorite haunt of local bird watchers since it attracts a variety of *Aves,* many of them very uncommon.

Smucker Studios

yet unnamed give a hint of what rose fanciers of the future will be growing. By the end of May, bearded irises, one of the Garden's specialties, display their countless colors on tall, strong stems. They are followed by colorful drifts of lilies, day lilies and gladiolus. The annual August auction of day lily and iris varieties draws large crowds to the Garden.

A collection of 30,000 annuals is set out each year chiefly in the areas bordering the Sunken Garden and Trellis Garden. Petunias, marigolds and snapdragons from the low-growing Floral Carpet series, to tall Rocket and Hit Parade varieties, bloom along with coleus and the excellent seed-grown "Carefree geraniums." Each variety of flower at Kingwood Center is carefully labeled for the information of gardeners who may want to try their hand at growing them at home. In one section of the center, test beds are maintained for current and forthcoming introductions of All-America Seed Selections.

Near the main entrance, the ravine path is a summer showplace for begonias of both the fibrous-rooted and tuberous-rooted varieties. Their lovely flowers are also displayed to great advantage in large hanging baskets.

In the fall, chrysanthemums take the prize for garden beauty at Kingwood Center, but they must still share their glory with other late-blooming beauties such as dahlias, asters, and the hardy colchicum. The last is a crocus-like charmer that overgrows its bounds, spreading wild and thick as Queen Anne's lace in the Ohio countryside. Sometimes called "autumn crocus," or "meadow saffron," the colchicum, with its purple and white flowers, does resemble the early spring crocus, but it is really a member of the lily family which takes its name from the ancient country of Colchis on the Black Sea.

In addition to tending the ever-changing display gardens, Kingwood Center also devotes considerable time and energy to testing more uncommon plants which will grow particularly well in Ohio gardens. Two of these are the spiny artichoke, well known to epicureans in this country, and the eremurus or "desert candle."

The artichoke, which many think of as a strange and foreign plant, is a relatively tolerant perennial which grows to a height of three and four feet here at Kingwood. In August its thistle-like blooms appear in a vibrant, eye-catching shade of blue. All artichokes are attractive, but those who wish to grow them for culinary purposes should obtain a tested strain, since some varieties may be tough and inedible.

From the name, "desert candle," the origin of this lovely member of the lily family (a relative of kniphofia, yucca, and aloe) is obvious. But it also grows well as a perennial in the less rigorous clime of Kingwood Center. The tall, strong flower spikes grow higher than a man's head. Of the three kinds grown here, the most popular is the variety Shelford with its pastel blooms. However, the waxy white flowers of *Eremurus himalaicus* and the pink *Eremurus robustus* also gain their share of attention.

The French Provincial King mansion,
now called Kingwood Hall, houses a library
that includes four hundred seed catalogues.

Below: On the north side of Kingwood Hall are two lead, eighteenth-century French statues. Pictured is one of them, the *Shepherd*.

Above: A dancing marble satyr and its offspring were imported from Italy and are one of the highlights of the Trellis Garden.

As fall progresses the magnificent hardwoods at the Kingwood Center make a display of color to rival the beauty of the fall flowers. Even after the leaves have fallen and the only flowers blooming at Kingwood are those in the greenhouses, the Center is still a place of lively activity. The annual Christmas Decorations Workshop arouses the interest of more than two thousand people. Each month the Kingwood Center bulletin, *Kingwood Notes*, is mailed to seven thousand families. This informative publication covers various aspects of the garden, lists new books at the library, provides helpful tips on growing plants and pest control, and even gives an occasional recipe. From the first flowers in spring until the grounds are blanketed with winter's snow, Kingwood Center is a place where the people of Mansfield, and visitors from everywhere, feel as much at home as they do in their own backyards.

Above: Kingwood Center's forty-seven acres include large expanses of lush, well-manicured lawns.

Right: Many birds at Kingwood are tame enough to offer an intimate view of bird life seldom seen even by hunters.

Belle Isle Park, Detroit, Michigan
ANNA SCRIPPS WHITCOMB CONSERVATORY
On the Island Once Called "The Swan"

Standing near a pot of Cattleya orchids
is a bronze statue symbolizing the
value of nature's pure water.

Opposite: A banana tree provides a
striking contrast with a silver palm
at Anna Scripps Whitcomb Conservatory.

One of the favorite features of Detroit's Belle Isle Park, in the middle of the Detroit River, is the Anna Scripps Whitcomb Conservatory. Although it has been here since the park was first constructed in 1904, only in recent years has the Conservatory gained its immense popularity.

In 1949, the two main wings and the central dome of the structure were completely rebuilt in glass and aluminum, with double glass at the top to ward off the blazing sun, and an entirely new heating and ventilating system to create a more suitable climate for the many exotic plants housed there. The large central dome, rising eighty-five feet into the air, is a landmark that can be seen for miles in any direction.

The Conservatory was dedicated in 1955 to Mrs. Anna Scripps Whitcomb, who had contributed generously to the cultural life of the city. Since that time, with the addition of many splendid orchids from the Whitcomb collection, the Conservatory's collection has become one of the best in the country.

Upon entering the Conservatory, the visitor first sees examples of plants from various parts of the building — a living table of contents. In the west wing is the Conservatory's magnificent orchid collection. These popular beauties bloom throughout most of the year, spreading their vivid colors of deepest purple to pure white across the landscaped stone terraces where they are displayed.

In the adjoining Tropical House, a variety of tropical fruit and flower-bearing plants create a lush, jungle-like setting. The fruit trees range from North American orange and lemons to the bananas, breadfruit, papayas, pomegranates and coffee trees. Against the greens of jungle foliage is a barrage of bright flower color. Here are the glowing reds of tropical hibiscus *(Hibiscus rosasinensis),* a large vine of waxen white stephanotis, the lovely fragrant yellow allamanda, the "cup of gold vine," *Solandra,* from Hawaii; and a panorama of other rich colors. All plants in the Conservatory are labeled for the visitor's information.

In the Palm House, under the high dome of the Conservatory, there is a variety of trees from around the world. More than a dozen of the largest palms reach toward the dome's peak. Occasionally one makes its way to the top and must be taken down before it pierces the glass. Most of the palms were transferred from Florida to Detroit for the dedication ceremonies in 1955. At the time this was the largest move of its kind ever undertaken in this country. Some of the trees weighed as much as three tons.

Outstanding in the tropical exhibits is
a pygmy date palm, which shares the room
with crotons and a common fig tree.

The *Opuntia* cacti produce mostly
yellow blooms which are succeeded
by a pulpy, edible fruit.

The Palm House opens onto the garden's Show House where there is a continuous floral exhibition. During Detroit's cultural season, six annual flower shows are held here and the finest of the many flowering plants grown by the city's horticultural department are displayed. The season begins with the Winter Show, from the second week in January to just before Easter. During the cold northern winter, the Conservatory offers a refreshing preview of cyclamen, cineraria, calceolaria, primroses and other gentle, warm-weather flowers set against a background of pink and white blossoming camellia trees.

The Easter Show, from the week before Easter to just before Mother's Day, brings traditional waxy white Easter lilies, heavy with beauty and fragrance, to highlight the displays of tulips, hyacinths, narcissus, genistas, azaleas and rhododendron. In the Mother's Day Show, giant pink, blue, and white hydrangeas, schizanthus, and marguerites are combined with the many colors of Martha Washington geraniums, a Mother's Day favorite.

During the warm summer months, the Show House is shaded to provide a cool, moist, glenlike setting for several varieties of fuchsias, caladiums, gloxinas, coleus and many other attractive and useful foliage plants. The Chrysanthemum Show, which ushers in the fall season, is one of the year's most popular attractions. Large standards of tall-stemmed giants, groupings of miniature chrysanthemums as well as daisy types, anemones and Japanese fujis are shown in colors ranging from gentle yellows to deep, rich golds and reds.

The cycle of seasonal color is completed with the Christmas Show where thousands of fresh blooming poinsettias in pinks, whites, variegated green and white, and rich red are combined with bright begonias and brilliant Jerusalem cherries.

It has been said that a visit to Whitcomb Conservatory is like a horticultural tour around the world. The Cactus Collection, next to the Palm House, offers a view of cactus and other succulents from the arid American West, South America and Africa. *Cereus* and other cactus varieties are grown here with agave, yucca and the interesting African aloes. In the Fernery, one can see not only the delicate American ferns, but also the Australian tree fern *(Alsophila australis)*, staghorn ferns *(Platycerium bifurcatum)*, and many others of this attractive plant family.

Outside the Conservatory, laid out among the lawns, are the sunken, formal gardens named for Henry T. Johnson, and a pool filled with colorful water lilies. The pool is surrounded by beds of perennials and the Rock Garden with its collection of fine miniature plants. Flower beds, framing the Conservatory's graceful lines, are hedged with clipped boxwood and yew, and set among groups of large hardwoods native to Michigan. The displays in these outdoor gardens remain constantly beautiful through three seasons of the year. Perennials and annuals are planted together and plants are changed regularly, sometimes as often as every seven to ten days. When one kind of flower fades from its peak of bloom it is replaced with another. But some flowers, like the hardy zinnia, are left to bloom throughout the long summer season.

The central dome of the Conservatory rises eighty-five feet into the air and is a landmark on Belle Isle Park.

This V-shaped bed features fuchsia in tree form and is surrounded by a low rock wall covered with English baby-tear.

In the Dahlia Garden, the biggest blossoms measure about fourteen inches of gorgeous color, while tiny bordering flowers are the popular button types. As new and improved varieties are developed through experiment and hybridization they are added each year.

From the formal gardens of the Conservatory one can see the Island's carillon bell tower, the band shell, and frequently the stack of one of the many freighters that pass up and down the river.

Originally called *Mah-nah-be-zee,* "the swan," by the Indians of Michigan, the Island now faces the skyscrapers of Detroit on one side and the city of Windsor, Ontario, on the other. For years the city of Detroit has been developing Belle Isle into a fine recreational park. An impressive 230 acres of virgin timber shelters a herd of wild deer and other wildlife. Lakes and ponds dot the Island and its shoreline offers a large sandy beach. During the summer months picnickers enjoy the sheltered inlets.

Michigan has more miles of exposed shoreline than any other state in the Union, and winter settles in with an iron grip. For the Anna Scripps Whitcomb Conservatory this is an important season. Water lilies for the pond must be carefully tended while the new root systems are developed. They are grown in special tanks so the plants will be well established for late spring displays. All orchid varieties require special temperatures, placement and care, although they are out of public view when not in bloom. In February the cannas are divided and placed in moistened sand on propagating benches. As they develop they are potted, and by the time spring weather arrives they are well established as ten-to-twelve-inch plants. The cold houses are kept at the temperature and humidity required to keep up plants that, while not tropicals or semi-tropicals, still require protection from the full impact of winter's harshness.

Inside the Conservatory, the plants grow much as they do in their native places. Every year the Winter Show and the Christmas Show draw record crowds to enjoy the spectacle of flowers brilliantly in bloom while the winter snows cover the ground. Through the modern techniques of heating and air conditioning, the color of the tropics can be enjoyed the year around on this island on the Canadian-American border.

The Conservatory lawns are decorated
with colorful beds surrounded by hedges
of clipped boxwood and yew.

Centralia, Missouri

CHANCE GARDENS

A Garden that Began as a Pastime

The toad's spurt of water nearly spans
the pond at the compact Chance Gardens,
which are 24,000 square feet in area.

Opposite: Looking from a Japanese pergola
with a red roof, one views two of the
many urns that decorate the Gardens.

There are countless numbers of Americans who consider backyard gardening one of the most relaxing and rewarding of all outdoor activities. From the patios of California, to suburban backyards in the Midwest and South, and apartment terraces and window gardens in the major cities of the East, an increasing number of gardeners take pleasure in the plants they grow. One of the early believers in this enjoyable pastime was A. Bishop Chance, who in 1907 founded the A.B. Chance Company, one of the country's major producers of power and communications line equipment.

In 1936 Bishop Chance decided to develop a garden in the backyard of his Centralia, Missouri, home. His interest in gardening continued and grew after his retirement from the business world. Although the area Mr. Chance chose for his garden is not large (only 24,000 square feet), and in no way compares to the hundreds of acres covered by numerous estates mentioned in this book, he used the available space to create a pleasant and refreshing setting.

The garden reflects its Midwestern location, but also reveals an Oriental influence in the use of stone, wood, water, trees and flowers, as well as in its architecture. The construction began with three hundred tons of native Missouri stone for the walks, walls and decorations. Mr. Chance once wrote to a friend: "I am . . . just one who enjoys and appreciates the geological wonders of our grand old state of Missouri and gains pleasure and happiness in their display in the assembly of our garden, that the ones passing this way may stop, rest, reflect and enjoy."

The Chance Gardens begin with an entry patterned in wood after the Japanese torii gate. From here, stone paths wend in different directions through the Gardens that include some 450 different kinds of flowers in their season. One leads to a rustic arbor with comfortable seats and one of the Gardens' many beautiful flower-filled urns. All through the Gardens there are attractive urns and other decorative accouterments, such as bird baths and sundials. In the background is the former residence of A.B. Chance and his family, now used as an accommodation for business guests of the A.B. Chance Company.

Over an arched bridge there is a pathway leading to one of the Gardens' main features, a Wishing Well and the Big Stone Arch. The arch is made of rugged Missouri stone, and flanked by two large urns. Beneath this massive arch, surrounded by tall evergreens and hardwoods, is the Wishing Well. Many of the ten thousand guests who visit the garden annually wish upon a coin as they toss it into the well. The tastefully planted flower beds display myriads of

The Gardens reveal an Oriental influence in the use of space, stone, wood, water, trees and flowers as well as in architecture.

roses, irises, marigolds and other well-known garden flowers combined with less usual garden companions such as silverweed *(Argentina anserina)* and cinquefoil *(Potentilla fruticosa)* with their delicate yellow flowers, and hypericum. Many lovely shrubs are planted to carry out the Oriental concept of the Gardens.

A shimmering stream with a small waterfall runs through the Gardens past banks of set stone and invitingly soft grass. There are bright-colored water lilies here and lotus, the sacred flower of Egypt. The stream can be seen from most parts of the garden and is one of the major features. Comfortable seats are situated along the banks to encourage quiet contemplation of the lovely colors, sounds and fragrances.

The charming pergola, constructed in Japanese style with a red roof, protects the entrance to a stone grotto built into the side of a hill and covered with grass and flowers. The Gardens maintain a delicacy and balance appropriate to their size.

Bishop Chance enjoyed his garden so much that he installed lights throughout so that its beauty could be enjoyed by night as well as in the daytime. Friends recall that on occasions when he got a phone call from business associates who arrived in town even at midnight, he would invite them over to the house for a guided tour of the Gardens.

Chance loved people as much as he loved flowers and never ceased to enjoy the many different visitors that the Gardens brought to his door. From May through October the Chance Gardens are open until 9:30 p.m. so that visitors can enjoy the spectacle of lights softening the enchanting beauty of the Gardens' many flowers. Even in the brook, underwater lights reveal the flashing movement of the many lively fish.

Mr. Chance, as one who built a company of his own, was a firm believer in our nation's free enterprise system. A plaque in the Gardens reads: "This garden was built and is maintained through the fruits of our American enterprise system. You are always welcome."

Bishop Chance's son, F. Gano Chance, succeeded his father as head of the company and continued his father's career of public service. In 1958, the Chance Foundation established annual scholarship awards for outstanding students in engineering or physical science, economics or teaching, and commercial studies. The foundation has also made many contributions to Centralia schools, the public library and other facilities. Yet the Chance Gardens remain a significant contribution to the community. Since A. Bishop Chance's death in 1949, they have been open as a public memorial to his generosity, industry and love of gardening. The people of Centralia, as well as the many visitors from far and wide, find here a refreshing and enjoyable spot of beauty. For gardeners in particular it is an inspirational example of the effects that can be attained even in a limited space.

St. Louis, Missouri

MISSOURI BOTANICAL GARDENS

The Evolution of a Renowned Midwestern Garden

In St. Louis, Missouri, housed in a transparent dome that appears to have dropped from outer space, there are tropical plants growing in a lush green profusion that closely resembles the deepest of untamed jungles. Giant palms, African tulips, figs and other spectacular exotics thrust upward almost seventy feet, while on the ground below, philodendrons, orchids, lianas and strangler vines compete for their share of the sun's filtered rays. To create this St. Louis "jungle," huge fans draw in unconditioned air from the outside, spray it with jets of cool or warm air, utilize it, and return it to the outside. A series of pneumatic controls in a Supervisory Data Center are programmed to regulate the air in every section of the planting.

The breathtaking steel-ribbed structure, covering a half acre of ground, is Missouri Botanical Gardens' famous Climatron. Completed in 1960, it was the first greenhouse ever built on R. Buckminster Fuller's principle of the geodesic dome. There are no bricks or beams to impede the light that floods in from every side. A quarter-inch layer of plexiglass separates the outside air with its changing temperatures from the stabilized and controlled air within. The Climatron has two levels to provide visitors with vantage points that would be impossible in a conventional greenhouse. The interior is arranged so one can walk through a series of simulated landscapes from India to Hawaii in less than an hour.

In the northeastern section of the Climatron the temperatures of the dry tropics are reproduced — warm days and cool nights such as one might find in parts of India. In addition to trees and flowers, there are rice paddies showing the grain in several different stages of development.

The western section of the Climatron is ten feet lower and ten degrees cooler. On the upper level is a pond, a tropical bog and a stream with a waterfall plunging over a rock cliff to a lower level. This popular area is dense with the foliage of semi-tropical fruit trees and plants. Pineapple, coffee plants, bananas, guavas, palms and papayas are planted here along with tree ferns, flowering ginger and bromeliads. Below the waterfall, in an area known as "Little Hawaii," the Climatron is programmed to evoke the cool days and warm nights of the gentle climate conducive to the growth of beautiful Hawaiian flowers. Nowhere else in the world is it possible to view so many marvels of the tropics all in one place.

Courtesy Missouri Botanical Garden

The Gardens grow their own hybrid water lilies in three large pools in front of the nine-year-old geodesic Climatron.

Opposite: For more than a century the Missouri Botanical Gardens have been world renowned for their horticultural contributions and botanical traditions.

Above: At the Hawaiian Waterfall, observant visitors are startled by a floating stone. It is a piece of genuine pumice, lava which cooled so quickly it is lighter than water.

Right: Red brick and green palms and ferns provide striking contrasts for the fine collection of orchids at the Botanical Gardens.

244

The horticulturists working in this extraordinary greenhouse are faced with the problems of tending a jungle. Plants grow so luxuriantly that a two-foot specimen can become a giant in several months. Pruning is a weekly necessity.

On special occasions at night the Climatron is lighted and the glowing transparent dome becomes an object of beauty in itself. So successful has the Missouri Climatron been that other gardens throughout the world are planning similar structures.

The Climatron, however, is not the only unique feature of the Missouri Botanical Gardens, nor is it the most famous. This garden, in a seventy-five-acre park in the center of busy St. Louis known to the city's residents as Shaw's Garden, maintains a reputation equal to that of the Royal Botanic Gardens at Kew and Jardin des Plantes in Paris, due to the contributions it has made to horticulture, natural science and botany since it opened to the public in 1889.

The Gardens were begun in the mid-nineteenth century, the project of a wealthy St. Louis businessman, Henry Shaw. An Englishman, he was born in Sheffield in 1800. At seventeen he was forced to leave school to help with the family business, and at eighteen he was sent to New Orleans to study the growing of cotton. From there he traveled up the Mississippi River to Missouri where, with $3,000 loaned him by an uncle, he began his own hardware business, outfitting immigrant trains traveling through St. Louis, "Gateway to the West." By the age of forty he had earned enough money to retire a wealthy man.

Mr. Shaw had no family and it became his mission in life to build a great botanical garden to benefit the citizens of his city of St. Louis. On a plot on the outskirts of town he built a home, Tower Grove House. Many of the pioneers that he outfitted for the westward trek sent him specimens of American flora from the dry desert regions and the Western mountains. With the aid of his close friend, Dr. George Engelmann, a famous St. Louis medical man and botanist, Shaw planned his garden. On the advice of Dr. Engelmann, Asa Gray of Harvard and Sir Joseph Hooker, later director of the Royal Botanic Gardens at Kew, the garden was started not with plants, but with a collection of fine books and the purchase of the great Bernhardi Herbarium from Europe.

The first permanent building was the museum that would house the herbarium and library. By 1909 the museum was too small for the growing collection and it was moved to a new building. The library contains 65,000 volumes, the earliest dating from 1437, and 100,000 pamphlets covering five centuries of botanical, horticultural and gardening writings.

The Bernhardi collection is one of the world's greatest botanical treasures. With over two million pressed and preserved specimens, it is one of the very few comprehensive collections of the plants of the world. An herbarium such as this allows researchers to study the evolution of plant life and its relationship to that of animals and humans. If visitors to the Gardens knew the excitement of the research that goes on here, they would be as impressed by the brick

Courtesy Missouri Botanical Garden

One of the cereus group, this attractive yet forbidding specimen, *Monvillea cavendishii*, is often used as stock for grafting.

245

Above: A quarter of a century ago, the Gardens were already famous for their fine orchid hybrids, such as this Black Thorpe Lady Slipper.

Opposite: This painted panel depicts Colombian mountains and valleys. It was painted in 1933 for Shaw's Garden's display at the First International Flower Show, held in St. Louis.

walls of the museum as by the most flamboyant flowers here.

Henry Shaw spent the last thirty years of his life developing his garden. When he died in 1889 the estate was turned over to a Board of Trustees, and the remains of his fortune were left to support the establishment which he named the Missouri Botanical Gardens. Shaw, in his lifetime, completely transformed the grounds of his estate, which were bare except for the single clump of sycamore trees still standing near the mausoleum. He built greenhouses, one of which, the Linnaean Greenhouse, is still used to house a fine camellia display. He planted formal gardens and lovely trees — euonymus, ginkgos, mulberries, bald cypresses and oaks — to line the paths which led to grassy knolls enclosed by stone fences and beautiful ironwork.

Since Henry Shaw's death, the Missouri Botanical Gardens have continued to maintain their position as one of the most important in the world through the continuing work of a group of well-known horticulturists. The funds that he left to the Gardens have been depleted over the years and it is now supported through a small admission charge and by gifts from local citizens who, quite deservedly, are taking increasing pride in it.

From December to March the greenhouse display features a choice collection of various varieties of camellias.

The original garden, created by Mr. Shaw, has been kept up and improved. The Linnaean Greenhouse still creates a Victorian backdrop of brick and glass for the Linnaean Garden in front of it. Designed to produce successive blooms with minimum labor, this garden is most beautiful in May when abloom with iris, peonies, foxglove and campanulas, and in June when colorful day lilies appear in profusion.

Experimentation with plants that grow in the Missouri area is a continuing project here. The Old Rose Garden, between the Linnaean Garden and the greenhouse, and the New Rose Garden, display a profusion of beautiful roses best suited to this climate.

One of the liveliest gardens here is the Herb Garden maintained by the St. Louis Herb Society. The fragrant herbs grow, showing their dark greens and olives contrasting with the background of an old-fashioned garden of tulips, daisies, zinnias and asters.

Between the main gate and the new Climatron, the water lily pools reflect the honeycombed dome and also display one of the finest collections of hybrid tropical water lilies in America. Nearly thirty-five new varieties of hybrid water lilies from the Missouri Botanical Garden have been distributed all over the world. Most of them were developed by the famous horticulturist George H. Pring. 'Missouri,' a night-blooming hybrid with flowering plants that often exceed twelve inches in diameter, thrives here.

In fall the dahlias, chrysanthemums and bright-leaved trees decorate the walks at Shaw's Garden. In November the annual Chrysanthemum Show, one of the finest in the Midwest, is held in the display house. In December there is a show of poinsettias here, and in the spring, a profusion of snapdragons, calceolarias, azaleas, cinerarias and cytisus.

In addition to the seventy-five acres in the city, the Gardens management operates a 1,600-acre arboretum at Gray Summit along U.S. Route 66 outside of town. Here, stretching along a mile of the Meramec River, are some fine stands of native timber and a large pinetum.

A quarter of a century ago, while Henry Shaw's garden was still in its infancy, the Missouri Botanical Gardens were already famous for their collection of fine orchid hybrids. Expeditions were sent to Colombia, Brazil, Panama and other tropical regions in search of these rare flowers. Today most of the orchid collection, still a famous one, is grown at the city garden.

Increasingly, as the Gardens expand and the townspeople become more interested in supporting them, the Missouri Botanical Gardens have come to function as an educational center for the St. Louis area. For adults there are courses in flower arrangement, herb gardening, plant propagation, the Japanese art of *bonsai*, as well as other subjects related to horticulture. For children from seven to sixteen, a free Saturday nature study program is offered nine months of the year with nature walks, films and other educational activities. And finally, the Gardens are used as a research center for undergraduate and graduate students in the area's colleges and universities.

Above: The poinsettia show is held during December. The traditional Christmas flower includes red, pink and white varieties.

Left: `Missouri` is a night-blooming hybrid water lily with flowers often exceeding twelve inches in diameter.

249

The Gardens have a "Master Plan for the Future," with which they expect to revolutionize the concept of botanical gardens. Starting with the Climatron in 1960, the scope of activities is broadened as funds become available. The direction of scientific work at the Gardens has varied with the times, ranging from an interest in the naming of flora of the developing West, and significant studies of the physiology of fungi, to plant hybridization, and more recently, plant hormones and climate control. Now once again research expeditions to the tropics are being conducted, and unusual new species are regularly returned to the greenhouses and gardens. The Gardens continue to produce a comprehensive study of the flora of Panama, and the herbarium still contains by far the most comprehensive collection of African flora to be found in the United States.

From all over the world archeologists and researchers send fossilized plant remains to the Missouri Gardens. Here Dr. Hugh Cutler, the Curator of Useful Plants, relates these fragments to a complex web of information provided by the Gardens' collection of beans, corn, squash and other important food plants. The oldest evidence of cultivated plants in the Americas (circa 600 B.C.) is here.

One of the most important projects in the plan for the future is a research building for graduate students in the field of botany. Here

Above: Tower Grove House, built in 1849, was the country home of Henry Shaw, the founder of the Missouri Botanical Gardens.

Below: The Spring Garden at one end of the greenhouse features peonies, irises and simple topiary accents.

The Linnaean House, a picturesque Victorian backdrop to the Old Rose Garden, is the oldest operating greenhouse in the United States.

will be housed the Gardens' famous historical collections. For now the National Council of State Garden Clubs, whose offices are here at the Missouri Botanical Gardens, has begun a project to furnish the reading and display rooms for the Gardens' library, and to recondition many of the fine old books.

The most revolutionary aspect of the new plan is a series of additions to Shaw's Garden which will make possible a display of plants from every climate in the world growing simultaneously. Visitors will be able to see plants from the Antarctic to Africa all within the space of this seventy-five-acre garden. The project has its start with the Climatron and the flanking buildings that now contain collections of plants from African and American deserts.

As it develops, this outstanding garden continues to follow the course established by its founder, Henry Shaw. Serving the nation and the world as a major repository of horticultural information and a leader of botanical research, it remains a place of surpassing peace and beauty.

251

Gage Park, Topeka, Kansas

REINISCH ROSE GARDEN
AND DORAN ROCK GARDEN

A Profusion of Roses

From earliest recorded history the jewel-toned blossoms of the rose have been treasured for their extraordinary beauty, fragrance and the many uses of their essential oils. The rose has served as a base for wines, preserves and other foods and as an ingredient in love potions. In recent years rose fanciers have become the largest organized group of flower growers in America, and their intense interest extends to an exchange of rose varieties and cultural information with other enthusiasts throughout the world.

Roses, of course, are a favorite for gardens and it would be supremely difficult to discover an American park or garden without them. The Reinisch Rose Garden in Topeka, Kansas, at the time of its construction in 1930, was one of the largest municipally owned rose gardens in the United States. Covering some ten acres in the southern section of Gage Park, it still retains its international fame as one of the country's finest all-around collections.

The garden was named for E.F.A. Reinisch, Topeka landscape architect who for thirty years was city Park Superintendent, and, before his death in 1929, developed the complete plans for the installation. Its construction was financed entirely from private contributions solicited by the Topeka Horticultural Society. Within sixty days after planting, the Garden was opened to the public. It was so outstanding that it immediately began attracting national attention. In 1932, only two years after its completion, the Garden won first prize in competition with 132 other cities and forty states in the "More Beautiful America Contest" sponsored by *Better Homes and Gardens* Magazine.

In the large, rectangular Rose Garden, under sunny Kansas skies, some three hundred varieties of climbers, floribunda, polyantha, hybrid perpetual and tea roses grow and thrive. There is a dazzling abundance of more than seven thousand rose bushes in all. The fragrant rectangular beds, most of which are planted with one variety of rose, are set about a lily-filled central pool dedicated to Thomas F. Doran, who headed the committee for the building of the Garden. Doran, a Topeka lawyer, raised funds for the Garden and also contributed so much of his own time and money that his fellow garden enthusiasts named both the Water Lily Pool and the nearby Doran Rock Garden in his honor.

The roses in the Reinisch Rose Garden and the adjoining Rose Test Garden are tended with the dedication and knowledgeable care that makes roses and other flowers flourish. Bob Foster, the Garden's Chief Horticulturist, is a man who believes he was born to

Many of the roses in the Test Garden will grow there for two years before being put on the market as a commercial flower.

Opposite: Funds from sponsors of Reinisch Rose Garden provided a new steel pergola constructed when the old wooden one was blown down by a strong wind in 1961.

The lovely pool and fountain were constructed in 1962 and dedicated to H. N. Richardson, a Garden sponsor.

The Rock Garden Lake is filled by two man-made streams. Below the lake is a miniature water mill.

grow flowers. A graduate of Kansas State University, he grew up on a farm near Topeka. Even as a child, he recalls, he surprised his teachers and fellow students by planting violets around their one-room schoolhouse.

When a rose bed is replaced in the Reinisch Rose Garden, all the soil is dug out to a depth of two feet in the fall. The roses are then planted in the spring and the hole is filled with a mixture of two parts good loam to one part leaf mold and one part well-rotted manure. Superphosphate and aluminum sulfate are added if soil tests indicate the need. The gardens are fertilized three times a year — once during the winter, once before the blooming season begins in April and finally in June. They are sprayed at least once a week and irrigated to a level of three inches by sprinklers turned on in the evening and set to run all night.

The beds in the largest section of the Reinisch Rose Garden are devoted to varieties made popular since 1930. There, in beds spaced two feet apart to allow for easy care and viewing, the rose fancier encounters many old friends. Here are the brilliant red of Charlotte Armstrong, a vigorous and popular hybrid tea rose, named after the distinguished mystery writer, and its forebear, the beautiful Crimson Glory, developed in Germany in 1935.

Outstanding, as it is in any garden, is the delicate-hued variety known as Peace, introduced in this country in 1945 by Robert Pyle. The story surrounding the flower — a series of striking coincidences — has almost become legend. One day in May 1945, as each of the major delegates to the United Nations Peace Conference in San Francisco returned to his hotel room, he found in a simple stem vase, a single pink-tinged, ivory blossom of the new rose, placed there by the American Rose Society. The rose then became a world-wide symbol for that very day, May 8, 1945, when joyous bells rang out to declare VE Day, the Allies' final victory in Europe.

Surrounding the central part of the Rose Garden, twenty-five beds of roses outline the history of the rose. One of the first among the ancient traditional flowers is *Rosa gallica officianalis,* the Apothecary rose, that flourished in Europe for hundreds of years before it was brought to America by the settlers of the Massachusetts Bay and Plymouth colonies. This beautiful deep pink rose, with its twelve-petaled, tulip-like blooms, ancestor of today's hybrid perpetuals, has run wild in the lanes and farmyards of New England.

The Napoleonic era saw the beginning of much of the current interest in rose hybridization. Empress Josephine loved all flowers, but particularly roses; and in the gardens of Malmaison, purchased by Napoleon in 1799, French horticulturists worked feverishly to develop new and exciting roses to please the imperial taste. It was here that André Dupont first discovered the value of hand-pollination of roses. His work was continued by his successor, Vibert, who is credited with the creation of most of the hybrid tea roses developed before 1850.

Two important roses of this period can be seen in the Reinisch Rose Garden: Harrison's Yellow — a hybrid which was introduced in 1830 and by 1849 had been transported over the plains around the

Colorful and dainty water lilies and other aquatic plants nearly pave the surface of the Rock Garden Lake.

255

Cape to California in time for the Gold Rush — can still commonly be found growing wild in the California countryside. The Mme. Hardy rose, introduced in 1832, is still considered by many to be the perfect damask rose. Its elegant white flowers conveniently reach their peak of bloom just before Mother's Day.

Another well-known ancient rose is Paul Neyron, a large-flowered hybrid perpetual introduced by A. Levet in 1869. Enthusiasts still argue over whether or not this deep pink, ruffled rose has a fragrance, but its fame is due mainly to the generous size of its blossoms and its relative lack of thorns.

Adjacent to the Reinisch Rose Garden is the Test Garden. As the All-America Rose Selections are made each year, they are planted in the Reinisch Test Garden, one of many throughout the country where their performance is carefully watched. Because many of the roses seen in the Test Garden will grow there for two years before being put on the market, rose lovers find it a good place to observe the growth of many varieties and compare them before buying. In the Test Garden and the Reinisch Rose Garden as many as 1,200 new plants are set out yearly to keep the gardens up to date. The funds for this yearly renovation are primarily furnished by interested individuals or civic groups. Such funds also provided a lovely pool with a fountain and a new steel pergola for the Garden to replace the wooden one blown down by a strong wind in 1961.

An immensely popular event each April is the Rose Show presented by the Topeka Rose Society. Awards are made to the best roses in several categories displayed in the Gage Park Shelter by rose enthusiasts from all over the state. Of course, the roses of the Reinisch Rose Garden, at their peak of bloom at that time of year, are a major attraction.

Just to the west of the Reinisch Rose Garden is the Doran Rock Garden, its internal flower-filled simplicity a sharp contrast to the symmetry of the Rose Garden. In this colorful little garden, more than ten thousand annuals are grown, not only for their beauty in this setting, but also to demonstrate their adaptability to the hot dry Kansas climate. The season begins with four hundred pansies followed by a display of thousands of tulips. The tulips, ranging through the color spectrum, grow amid the hundreds of truck loads of rock brought to the garden when it was built in 1930. After their blooming season each year, half the tulips are dug out and replaced by flowering annuals. A massive display of chrysanthemums ends the season.

The Rock Garden Lake is filled by two man-made streams and is surrounded by large shade trees. One of the streams, which flows over a four-foot wall into a pond where youngsters can wade on hot days, is a special delight of children. Below the pond is a wishing well and a miniature water mill made of native limestone. The water flows past the turning mill wheel and under a bridge to the lake that is filled with water lilies and other aquatic plants. The people of Topeka have good reason to be proud of this municipal park with so much of interest to both children and adults. And it is a pleasant stop for any travelers in the area.

In 1932 the Garden won first prize in competition with 132 other municipally owned gardens in forty states.

Opposite: The water lily pool at Reinisch is named after T. F. Doran, chairman of the committee which initiated the Garden.

257

Woodward Park, Tulsa, Oklahoma

TULSA MUNICIPAL ROSE GARDEN

An Outstanding Terraced Rose Garden

Originated in 1934 by the Tulsa Garden Club, the Tulsa Municipal Rose Garden was designed by landscape architect C. Burton Fox.

Opposite: Among the nine thousand roses at the terraced gardens are these Mister Lincolns, huge, fragrant, perfect for cutting.

Along with the development of garden clubs in this country, and the growing awareness of the need for action, an increasing number of horticulturists, garden enthusiasts and civic-minded men and women have made countless contributions to city beautification projects, parks and public gardens. One of the most outstanding projects of this sort is the Tulsa Municipal Rose Garden, originated in 1934 by the Tulsa Garden Club and developed and cared for today by the Tulsa Park and Recreation Department.

The project began inauspiciously enough at a club meeting with a discussion on roses chaired by a well-known local rosarian, Arthur Truex. So intense was the interest in the subject among the members, that they were alerted by the Superintendent of the city's Park Department, W.O. Doolittle, to a project under consideration for a formal garden in the city's Woodward Park. One terrace of this garden, Doolittle said, could be planted with roses.

With the encouragement of the chairman of the rose garden project, Mrs. F.W. Higgens, the club soon had evolved an even more ambitious plan — a plan that the entire Woodward Park garden be given over to a display of roses. A sum of $1,200 a year was set aside from club funds for the purchase of roses for the four-and-a-half-acre garden which was designed by landscape architect C. Burton Fox.

The first roses were planted in the Tulsa Municipal Rose Garden in 1935. Two years later the Tulsa Garden Club received the *Better Homes and Gardens* Magazine bronze plaque for their efforts. Through the years the Garden has been praised by such renowned rosarians as America's Dr. J. Horace McFarland and Harry Wheatcroft of England who said it was of the finest design, as well as the best maintained garden that he had seen in the United States. In addition to continued club support, rose growers throughout the country have been generous in donating the best of their established favorites and new hybrids for display, so that today the Garden is a remarkable collection of new and old rose varieties. Thousands of visitors take delight each year in the scent and sight of the spectacular flowers — a kaleidoscopic display of color that lasts from early May until late October, although the blooming season reaches its first peak in mid-May and a second one in October.

The upper terrace begins at the top of a gentle incline to the east and the remainder of the Garden falls gradually in five other terraces to the street level some nine hundred feet below. Stone

A Peace rose, one of the most popular varieties, was given to each major delegate at the United Nations Peace Conference.

Canaert junipers, such as these on the second and third terraces, serve as staid accents to the brilliant rose colors.

steps lead from the top of the Garden to the street. A series of fountains, shallow pools, ornamental shrubs and shade trees provide a pleasant background and a look of cool spaciousness. Ivy-covered retaining walls separate the terraces that are bright with the color of nine thousand roses.

Along the east side of the highest terrace are trellises filled with bright climbing roses. A small pool lies on each side of the central walk, and several Southern magnolia trees, with their luxurious creamy-white flowers in May and June, brighten the sides of the terrace. In the fall the dominant color here is the brilliant red of the berries of the twelve-foot-high deciduous hollies, called possum-haw *(Ilex decidua)*. They are planted at the far corners of the pools.

Among the roses on this terrace are the climbing varieties of Charlotte Armstrong, Chevy Chase, Tiffany, Chrysler Imperial, Royal Gold and Bloomfield Courage. They augment a display that includes Dainty Bess, often known as the queen of single roses, an orchid-pink rose with large soft petals; Helen Traubel, 1952 All-America Rose Selection; and the pink-tinged Peace, probably the most popular variety in the world.

The graceful, oval main entrance, bordered with burford holly *(Ilex cornuta burfordi)*, opens to the second level, the largest of the terraces. The terrace's focal point is the large pool in its center surrounded by many popular rose varieties. K.A. Victoria, a familiar white rose, was introduced in 1891 by the famous rose breeder, P. Lambert. The bright color of Harrison's Yellow, a popular hybrid *foetida*, has been well known in this country since the Gold Rush days of 1849. The brilliant red Americana and the bi-color Forty Niner, with petals of Chinese red and chrome yellow, are but two of the many beautiful hybrid tea roses to be seen.

Hybrids excel on the second terrace with the enormous coral pink blooms of South Seas and the hot orange color of Tropicana bright in contrast with the elegant white buds of Matterhorn and the fragrant yellow flowers of Mrs. P.S. du Pont. On this terrace, too, we find the magnificent grandiflora, Queen Elizabeth, with its huge, soft pink flowers; the 1940 All-America Rose Selection, World's Fair; and the beautiful Soeur Therese that was introduced by French rose breeders in 1930.

On the third terrace, Sam McGready, a famous rose breeder, is recalled through a sampling of his roses — McGready's Sunset, McGready's Yellow, with its distinctive buttercup shade, and one of the all-time favorites of American rose growers, Mrs. Sam McGready. Several All-America Rose Selections are found here including the bright red of grandiflora Scarlet Knight, and the lovely pink Miss All-American Beauty, a hybrid tea rose. Red and white dominate the color scheme here with the red beauty of Crimson Glory, the White Knight, and a famous climber, Frau Karl Druschki, a white hybrid perpetual. The pool on this level nestles at the foot of the upper terrace wall, and a charming view of the placid water and the terraces beyond and below is provided from behind the wrought-iron railing above the pool.

Opposite: The spacious setting and largeness of the Garden, as well as its formal terraced nature, create an Italian Renaissance effect.

The pools at Tulsa Municipal Rose Garden, such as this one on the second terrace, are made of limestone rock and concrete.

Opposite: Each terrace presents a kaleidoscopic display of color that lasts from early May to late October.

On the fourth and fifth terraces, roses of a more recent origin create a gorgeous array of pinks and reds, lavender, orange, white, yellow and gold. Two 1969 All-America Rose Selections are located on the fourth terrace — the clear pink floribunda, Gene Boerner, and the brilliant orange-red of the double-blooming grandiflora Comanche. The sixth and final terrace has a Y-shaped walk leading to the street level.

In addition to the Tulsa Municipal Rose Garden, Woodward Park contains one of the nation's twenty-three rose test gardens that are sponsored by the American Rose Society. Under the direction of Arthur Truex, who first initiated the Tulsa Garden Club's interest in roses, and, since 1964, of Homer Spencer, the garden contains new rose varieties — identified only by number — that are closely studied for two years or more before being put on the market. The Tulsa Municipal Rose Garden also displays some of these fledgling roses which may be the All-America Rose Selections of tomorrow.

The Tulsa Garden Club itself has prospered and grown in the years since it started the Rose Garden, and many of its members are now involved in the lectures, workshops and flower shows at the Tulsa Garden Center, located next to Woodward Park. A fine library offers facilities for horticultural research. Yet the project that most brings pride to Tulsans is their Municipal Garden, where each year the beauty of thousands of blooms stands in tribute to an idea, and the combined efforts of dedicated garden lovers to fulfill their dream of a magnificent planting of roses.

WHITE SHADOWS

An Artist's Singular Creation

The garden contains numerous separate niches in which stand Chinese marble figures, saints and sages, some graceful, some grotesque.

Opposite: At White Shadows, flaming red azaleas withstand the blazing Texas sun as well as the biting cold of winter.

A singularly beautiful and noteworthy garden is the dream of many a home gardener, but for one man it is a difficult task and there are few people with the time or patience to create a showplace. Very few are the private gardens to compare with White Shadows, the Texas home of one of the century's most famous portrait artists, Douglas Chandor.

Chandor, an Englishman by birth, was just seventeen when World War I broke out in Europe. He enlisted in the First Life Guards and later became an officer in the Scottish commando regiment, the Lovat Scouts. It was here that the young Chandor first tried his hand at portraiture, doing sketches of his fellow guardsmen. When he was mustered out at the end of the war with a medical discharge and a metal pin in his knee resulting from a wound, Chandor decided to attend the Slade School in London.

In a matter of years Chandor had become one of the best known portrait artists on the Continent. He had dreamed of seeing America ever since his father, who was once a law student at Harvard, had told him about it years before. When Joseph Duveen, the well-known art dealer, offered to introduce him to art dealers and artists in America, he jumped at the chance. Before long he was doing his series of now famous portraits which include such prominent individuals as Andrew Mellon, Eleanor Roosevelt (the only portrait of her ever painted), Speaker of the House Sam Rayburn, Winston Churchill, Bernard Baruch and other such notables.

In 1934 Chandor married Ina K. Hill, a girl from Weatherford, Texas, and settled down to live in that state. Chandor loved the sunny hot land of his new home, but deplored the lack of gardens, and so decided to create one of his own. He designed what was surely one of the most difficult to build and one of the most beautiful one-man gardens in all of gardening history. His basic ideas were drawn from the study of both European and Oriental gardens. Significant aspects from the history of garden design were combined in Chandor's imagination with the unique freshness of his own artistic spirit.

The soil that Chandor had to work with was caliche, a composition of shells from the ancient seas that once covered this land and baked to the consistency of hardened cement by the blazing Texas sun. Before beginning to cope with this, the artist designed his garden completely and built a scale model. Then with dynamite, pickaxe, mules and a tremendous amount of hard labor, he began to make holes for shade trees, mostly oaks and rock elm.

Into the rocky hillside he blasted a channel for a stream that would water the garden.

To grow a garden in the extremes of the Texas climate meant searching out the plants that could withstand not only intense heat, but also the biting cold of Texas winters. Fortunately these happen to include such beauties as azaleas, wisteria, magnolia, Texas roses, crape myrtle and hydrangea. The house, white-painted brick with a tiled roof reflecting the area's Spanish heritage, was nestled into the center of the garden. The total environment was artfully conceived as a whole, and was a tremendous undertaking. It was a labor of love that lasted for sixteen years. With the help of his wife Ina, who also kept his books, wrote letters, entertained his famous clients and packaged his paintings for shipping, Chandor built fountains and garden sculptures, walks and seven acres of flower beds. By 1953, when Douglas Chandor was taken by sudden death, the plans so carefully drawn in 1936, were almost completed.

Entering White Shadows through tall, white, wrought-iron gates, you discover a land of artful fantasy. The top of the uphill drive brings every visitor to a halt at the breathtaking sight of a mountain — forty feet of weathered stones, many weighing fifteen tons or more, hauled in one by one from far and wide. The craggy, rock "mountain," covered with a growth of moss and pines, creeping vines and flaming pink azaleas, was Douglas Chandor's last project and is not yet completed. Its cave and green lagoon still wait for the waterfall that was to have plunged down to the nearby Chinese water gardens.

Above: The Gray Garden was once a sun pit where nothing grew, but now it sparkles with pink climbing roses, yarrow and lavender anthemis.

Opposite: Douglas Chandor used dynamite, a pickax and tireless labor to blast and carve his garden into the rocky terrain.

Below: Tall squared hedges of cherry-laurel and a low stone wall studded with colorful rock-plants accentuate the formal Bowling Green.

Azaleas are found throughout the garden —
at the Bowling Green pool, along walkways and
near the lagoon in front of the house.

Opposite: Around the Chinese Pool is a
clipped hedge of white azaleas. An acre of
trained wisteria spreads itself above.

Across the drive a number of mythical animals made from large rocks surround a circular pool filled with water flowers and goldfish. Millstones are used for stepping-stones across the pond, and at the far side, a Chinese junk lies anchored, made entirely of rock and covered with blossoms. Nearby, a grotto of caliche protects Chinese marble figures.

The Chandor house is not visible through the garden's greenery until you practically stumble upon it. The front of the house faces east across a flower-filled lagoon spanned by the delicate arch of a white Chinese bridge. Around the lagoon and the front of the house, tall shade trees fill the bright days with the rustle of leaves and cool green shadows. There are colorful azaleas here, and potted plants. The sinuous branches of wisteria spread their great clusters of purple flowers overhead. Chinese lanterns and a miniature Chinese temple complete an artist's haven of cool seclusion. This is an exceptionally inspiring feature to others who live in a similar hot dry climate.

Across the Chinese bridge, a corridor of living bamboo arches over a tiled walk that leads to the English Bowling Green. To the left a garden gate opens onto the Boxwood Garden, a secluded "room" sheltered by tall cedar elms. Unclipped boxwoods surround a small, tiled pool centered with an urn full of flowers and a marble statue — a delicate totally British garden. Douglas Chandor came here daily to meditate in the stillness of this tiny garden, also visible from the windows of his studio.

The Bowling Green, stretching its length from a stone terrace adjoining the house, is another thoroughly European touch. It is as British as any eighteenth-century garden in England. The beauty of the long green lawn suggests the labor required to blast and dig out two feet of caliche and replace it with the more fertile soil that good grass must have. Tall squared hedges of cherry-laurel *(Prunus laurocerasus)* and a low stone wall studded with colorful rock-plants accentuate the clipped freshness of the lawn. At the end of the Bowling Green is a pool surrounded by lilacs, azaleas and colorful weeping crape myrtle trees. The elves and tiny animals guarding the pool might have come directly from an English fairy tale.

The lagoon becomes a stream with lotus and water lilies and small islands with sculptured temple pagodas and Chinese water birds. A path beside the stream leads to an azalea-bordered walkway under the leafy shade of wisteria. From here you can see the back of the Chandor house and one of the favorite areas in all of White Shadows, the Gray Garden. This was once a trouble spot, a sun pit where nothing would grow. Finally, after trying many plants, Chandor discovered that plants with gray foliage could successfully withstand the hot Texas sun. Now a circle of gray senecio filled with yellow yarrow and lavender anthemis are surrounded by hedges of crape myrtle and a pergola of pink climbing roses. At twilight the silver-blue of senecio blends into the blue of the twilight sky. Douglas and Ina Chandor loved to sit in this garden in the evening and watch the colors change and fade.

Beside a brick path here, is a marker with the Latin inscription: "May the Little Garden Flourish. Dedicated to Ina." How well it

The ornamental iron entrance gates open into a long, uphill driveway lined with colorful Lady Banksia yellow roses.

The front of the Chandor house faces east across a flower-filled lagoon spanned by the delicate arch of this white Chinese bridge.

did flourish is apparent as the next few steps lead to a pleached *allée* of pear and apricot trees and then to a lovely sunken garden growing in what was once a dry canyon. Arched overhead, the branches of the fruit trees bend with blossoms in the spring, and with their harvest in the autumn. Flowers grow in the low stone wall edging the *allée*.

At the base of the brick stairways which Douglas Chandor struggled to build, one enters a garden wonderland. At its entrance between the brick stairways, a tiny niche made of colored marbles protects a statue of Kuan-Yin, the Chinese goddess of peace. In the center of this garden is a tiled pool bordered with white azaleas. (The Chandors made the tiles and baked them in their kitchen oven.) And in the pool a Chinese fountain with ornately carved Ming dragons shoots jets of water twenty feet into the air. Around the circular walk and stone walls are masses of flame and pink azaleas, but overhead is the crowning glory of White Shadows. Above the water on a web of fine wires, the pendant clusters of pink and purple wisteria spread a graceful canopy of color against the bright spring sky. And in the still water, the entire panorama is reflected as in a mirror.

Ina Chandor, since her husband's death, has devoted her time to keeping up the garden at White Shadows. By charging a modest admission fee she hopes to complete her husband's still unfinished project, the "mountain" and its waterfall. More than fame or his distinguished portraits, Douglas Chandor cherished this garden. His work was a labor of love. It stands as an inspiring example of what can be accomplished with wood, stone, water and living plants — in the hands of an artist.

Opposite: Two small grottoes of volcanic rock, studded with ferns, geraniums and bougainvillea, decorate the garden.

San Marino, California
HUNTINGTON BOTANICAL GARDENS
A Rare and Beautiful Garden

In 1904 Henry E. Huntington hired a young horticulturist, William Hertrich, to develop and landscape his estate.

Opposite: A laughing bronze statuette, *Bacchante,* by Frederick MacMonnies, presides over the rockery at Huntington Gardens.

In 1892 Henry E. Huntington first saw the spectacular view from the San Marino Ranch — to the north across the majestic Sierra Madre Range to Mt. Wilson and Mt. Lowe, and on clear days, the lofty summit of Mt. San Antonio; and to the south, rolling acres of sun-soaked orchards and the blue haze of the Whittier Hills. He was a guest of the J. de Barth Shorb family. He was so taken with the site, that ten years later, after de Shorb's death, he bought it for his California home. In 1904 he hired a young horticulturist, William Hertrich to develop and landscape the estate. This period of the Gardens' history is delightfully recounted in Hertrich's book *The Huntington Botanical Gardens 1905-1949.*

Mr. Huntington was one of the country's wealthiest and most important businessmen at that time. His enterprises included railroad lines connecting the Atlantic and Pacific coasts, electric railroads throughout California, land companies, and shipyards at Hampton Roads. But busy as he was, before the Huntington home was built in 1914, he loved to visit his San Marino property. He was particularly interested in the garden work and, Mr. Hertrich recalls, would lean on his cane watching for hours while some area was planted or a big tree was moved.

Near the southeastern edge of the property, growing in an arid facsimile of desert land, is the Desert Garden, the first important botanical collection conceived for the new estate. This grouping was one of William Hertrich's favorite projects but Mr. Huntington had little use for the prickly plants. His attitude was colored by his first experience with them while he was supervising work on the Southern Pacific Railroad. In stepping back to let some grading equipment pass by, he directly encountered a spiny cactus. Hertrich, nevertheless, continued the collection, and eventually even Mr. Huntington was enthused enough to show visitors through its winding paths. It now covers ten acres and is the largest assemblage of mature specimens of cactus and other succulents in the world. Many of the plants were brought here full grown from Mexico, Africa and South America.

The Desert Garden presents an intriguing combination of strange forms in shades of green, brown and red combined with the colors of cactus blooms in the spring and summer. The fascinating flowers of other succulents, particularly the South African aloes, bloom throughout most of the rest of the year. Outstanding among the varied kinds are the massive five-ton *Cereus xanthocarpus,* many

Gottscho-Schleisner, Inc.

Photos: Courtesy Huntington Library

At the far end of the North Vista is an Italian Renaissance fountain. On each side of the Vista are seventeenth-century stone figures brought from a garden in Padua.

varieties of the Mexican pincushion cactus, tall South African aloes with their spires of red buds, *Cephalocereus senilis,* or the old man cactus of Mexico, so-called for its long white hairs, and the towering *Carnegiea gigantea* from the Arizona desert.

Adjoining the Desert Garden is the beautiful Palm Garden with two hundred specimens from all over the world, and nearby, the colorful and dramatic Lily Ponds. Past the ponds one enters an entirely different world of carefully arranged gardens whose spacious green lawns and pathways are shaded by tall trees. The scene is dominated by the cooly elegant white facades of the library and the Huntington Art Gallery, once the Huntington home. From here is the spectacular view of the San Gabriel Valley that first attracted the owner.

Both the Art Gallery and the library are famous in their own right. The San Marino home was built to withstand fire or earthquake, and it was here that Mr. Huntington chose to keep most of his magnificent art collection. The collection, now on display at the gallery, includes a number of outstanding eighteenth- and early nineteenth-century British paintings with representative works of Reynolds, Gainsborough, Lawrence, Romney, Turner and Constable. *Pinkie* by Sir Thomas Lawrence, *Sarah Siddons as the Tragic Muse* by Sir Joshua Reynolds, and Thomas Gainsborough's *Blue Boy* are among the best known. The gallery also contains several Boucher tapestries, a notable collection of Renaissance bronze statuettes, furniture, clocks, porcelains and silver.

The library building, finished in 1920, now has one of the finest existing collections of British and American history and literature. In addition, it contains such treasures as a *Gutenberg Bible* printed in Mainz about 1450-1455, hand-illuminated Books of Hours, first editions of Chaucer's *Canterbury Tales,* the original manuscript of Benjamin Franklin's *Autobiography* in his own hand, and thousands of other rare and valuable items. In one wing of the library is the Arabella D. Huntington Memorial Collection of fifteenth- and sixteenth-century Italian and Flemish paintings and eighteenth-century French furniture, tapestries, sculpture and porcelains.

Mr. Huntington loved southern California and the San Marino Ranch more than any of his other homes. But since his second wife Arabella favored New York and Paris, he had to convince her that California was not a wilderness. The interior of the Huntington home, finished in 1914, was designed with a seventeenth- and eighteenth-century English elegance. Every effort was made to create a beautifully finished landscape. Full grown trees were planted on the lawns. This was accomplished by using nursery-grown specimens of redwood, incense and Himalayan cedars, pepper trees and other trees planted as early as 1905, and also by

Above: The view from the South Terrace of the Art Gallery includes a *tempietto* inhabited by no less than Louis XV being guided by Love.

Below: The Shakespeare Garden with its English sundial and the sculptured bust of its patron is reminiscent of Elizabethan days.

transplanting full grown trees from other Huntington property. This was the first such operation ever carried on in the United States. The trees moved included many large palms, a large *Magnolia grandiflora* with two trunks, and cedar trees.

William Hertrich has many amusing tales to tell about these tree-moving ventures. Since the time was 1910-1914, the trees were carried by horse-drawn wagons, or shipped by rail to the private San Marino spur. One day while pulling a heavy tree through the city of Los Angeles, the truck got stuck and the workmen had to dig a hole in the city street to get it out. As Hertrich's men were digging, the city's street inspector passed by. He took the embarrassed Hertrich into custody, but the matter was finally settled over a glass of beer. The inspector let Hertrich go with the cool warning that although Mr. Huntington owned much land in Los Angeles County, he did not own the city streets.

To the west of the Huntington home are the formal gardens. The Rose Garden, planted in 1907 before the house was built, now spans one end of the West Lawn. Banked on trellises and in beds across the lawn, more than a hundred varieties of roses seduce the senses with color and fragrance. When the Huntingtons lived here, there was an aviary next to the Rose Arbor with a large collection of caged birds. On another part of the grounds, ducks, swans and other waterfowl swam on a pond where Mr. Huntington loved to come with his grandchildren.

Above: In the Oriental Garden, winding paths and the steep Moon Bridge lead among Japanese wisteria, dwarf maples and cycads.

Opposite: The Sand and Rock Garden is part of the Japanese Garden. One of the newest areas of the Gardens, it was opened in November 1968.

The Herb Garden includes a large collection of culinary herbs interspersed with rare and beautiful shrubs and trees. In the Shakespeare Garden, crowned with a bust of the Bard, there is an interesting variety of the trees and flowers mentioned in his works, and accompanied by an appropriate quote. Between the Rose Garden and the Herb Garden is an arbor, which in season, is covered with the colorful flowers of wisteria, clematis and jasmine.

There are magnificent views from both the north and south sides of the Huntington mansion. The North Vista, at the front of the mansion, extends down a wide lawn lined with seventeenth-century statues of mythical and allegorical figures from a garden in Padua and ends with a magnificent Italian marble fountain framed by a backdrop of mountains. Paths on either side are shaded by tall oak trees through plantings of camellias, azaleas and rhododendron.

The South Terrace faces the San Gabriel Valley, the snowy peaks of San Gorgonio, Cucamonga Peak, and "Mt. Baldy." To the west is a decorative Roman Temple shaded with Montezuma cypress. To the east is the Gardens' magnificent collection of cycads, which includes venerable specimens hundreds of years old.

Mr. Huntington collected a large number of statues, garden ornaments and miscellaneous pieces of art that, to the dismay of his staff, he loved to rearrange until he had found precisely the right place for them. Not infrequently was an object thought to be safely settled in the garden replaced soon afterward by something Mr. Huntington considered more attractive.

The oak tree was Mr. Huntington's favorite of all the trees, shrubs or flowers. He all but fired one of the surveyors at San Marino Ranch for driving a surveyor's spike into a tall old oak. So intense was his feeling for these trees that it prompted the first major tree surgery in this country, carried out on a pair of ancient oaks near the Rose Garden which had been blown down by storm.

Opposite: The Desert Garden: dun earth, gray and sienna rocks, dull greens and slaty blues with an occasional orange or crimson fruit and fluted columns and ribbed shafts rising against the sky.

Below: The forbidding desolateness of a desert shows clearly in these cacti with their vicious thorns and prickles.

There are few places in the United States that contain as much of the rare and beautiful as Huntington Botanical Gardens.

Opposite: The Desert Garden Road leads to the largest collection in the world of mature desert plants growing out of doors.

Down the hill from the Rose Garden, in what was once an old ravine and reservoir, is the Japanese Garden, the greatest triumph of engineering on the estate. Mr. Huntington wanted something done with the unsightly canyon before he moved, and this garden was built in less than six months in 1912. The task would have been impossible had Hertrich not discovered in nearby Pasadena a complete Japanese nursery for sale, including a Japanese house which was being used as a commercial tearoom. The house and its fine collection of Oriental flora were moved almost intact to San Marino. Today it is a relaxingly gentle glade with splashing waterfalls and a stream with an arched Oriental bridge. There are lovely banks of azaleas, Chinese and Japanese wisteria, blossoming cherry trees, dwarf maples, camellias, ferns, pine and cycads. The impressive torii gate at one entrance, a massive and traditional religious structure shipped from Alaska, sets the character of the garden. A brass bell in an enclosure built entirely without nails by a Japanese workman sends forth its sonorous tones.

On the far side of the canyon, a Japanese house, a replica of a seventeenth-century samurai's dwelling, is lighted and open to viewing. Authentic Japanese mats, screens, scrolls, carvings, a tea service and fresh flower arrangements convincingly imply that the family has only stepped out for a while.

The camellia has long been a favored plant in the Orient, and in the Japanese Garden area is a fine collection of rare *Camellia reticulata* imported from China where they were first cultivated for the size and beauty of their flowers. The Camellia Garden, opened in 1951 as a test garden for the American Camellia Society, stretches through seven acres of hillside. With some 1,500 varieties of camellias, primarily *Camellia japonica*, it is an unsurpassed showcase for this wonderful flower.

On the road running from the North Vista through a grove of oranges and avocados, is the family mausoleum designed by John Russell Pope, whose most famous work is the Jefferson Memorial in Washington, D.C. The avocado grove flanking the road to the mausoleum produced the first commercial avocados grown in California.

Mr. Huntington, who had enjoyed some of this exotic fruit at the Jonathan Club, where he stayed in Los Angeles, got some seeds from the club kitchen. He took them to San Marino Ranch where the seeds were started, nurtured and planted in the gardens. Such experimentation to test growing conditions in southern California has included hachiya and Fuya persimmons, Chinese jujubes, wine and table grapes, pistachios and pecans, as well as Mexican and Central American fruits such as bananas, mangoes, pineapples, sapotas, guavas and papayas.

The town of San Marino, now an expanding metropolis, was incorporated in 1913 by Henry Huntington and several of his friends. When he died in 1927, his deed of trust specified that the two-hundred-acre botanical gardens, along with the library and Art Gallery should be opened for the benefit of the people of San Marino and for the rest of the world. There are few places in the United States that contain as much of the rare and beautiful as one finds assembled at the Huntington Botanical Gardens.

La Canada, California

DESCANSO GARDENS

Color-Laden Sanctuary in Southern California

Courtesy Descanso Gardens

The Far Eastern motif of the Gardens spreads throughout the area surrounding the teahouse in the Oriental Pavilion.

In its English translation *descanso* means, "where I rest." No truer name could be given to this picturesque garden set in a natural bowl among the verdant San Rafael Hills. To the people of Los Angeles County, which is rapidly being bulldozed into subdivisions, Descanso Gardens has become what its name signifies, a place of rest and relaxation where it is still possible to enjoy the peace, quiet and grandeur of nature. "The People" have a special interest in Descanso. It was only through the efforts of a small group of concerned citizens that these beautiful gardens were saved from public auction in 1958.

The 165 acres that is now Descanso Gardens began its recorded history in 1784 as part of a land grant to José Maria Verdugo from Governor Pedro Fages of California. The grant was known as Rancho San Rafael. During the nineteenth century, gold was discovered at Rancho San Rafael and a mining camp was built, but soon closed. Today all that remains of this dream of instant wealth are a few stone foundations. In the 1840's Rancho San Rafael was divided, 5,745 of its acres becoming Rancho La Cañada.

In the early 1930's, Manchester Boddy, a wealthy Los Angeles publisher, discovered the overgrown and unused land while on a weekend nature walk with his sons. Impressed by its beauty, he had some of it cleared and built a house surrounded by woods and the hills. During the sixteen years that followed, more than a hundred thousand camellias were planted in the woodlands in sight of the house. Though camellias were not popular in America at that time, he imported varieties from China, Japan, Europe and the American South, including the difficult-to-grow *C. reticulata*, recently imported from China.

Another of Boddy's favorite flowers was the rose. In 1948 he asked one of America's most important rose specialists, Dr. Walter Lammerts, to design a rose garden for Descanso. The garden which Dr. Lammerts created became the famous History of The Rose Garden, which accurately traces the history of this favored flower from pre-Christian times to the present.

The Descanso Gardens were opened to the public in 1951. In 1953, the County of Los Angeles bought them from Boddy for $1.4 million, but they were poorly attended. Few people had heard of them, and the interest they generated was slight. Therefore, the county decided to auction the land for subdivision. A handful of local citizens, calling themselves the Descanso Gardens Guild, who understood the value of public gardens to this rapidly growing area,

Opposite: Flowing the length of the live oak grove at Descanso is a crystal-clear stream descending from a spring in the hills.

The stately woodlands were about to be auctioned for subdivision when a group of local citizens intervened to save them.

Opposite: More than 500,000 people each year travel the forest trails that are lined with masses of flaming bright colors.

made an eloquent plea that Descanso Gardens be given another chance. Their request was granted, and work began to expand the scope of the plantings and make the public more aware of them.

Due to the concern of these few dedicated individuals and their unremitting work to preserve Descanso's beauty, the Gardens have become a famous landmark in the Los Angeles area. More than 500,000 people each year travel its woodland trails and enjoy the beauty of massed camellias, azaleas, roses and the other beautiful flowers that bloom there.

Of the Gardens' 165 acres, thirty of the most centrally located are devoted to the shade-loving plants such as camellias, azaleas and rhododendron. In these acres, the hot California sun is filtered through the leafy lattice-work of ancient California oaks to create the green translucence of forest shade. Ten thousand varieties of rhododendron, along with the Gardens' thousands of camellias, stud the forest paths with brilliant hues of pink and orange, purple and white. The elegant camellias, planted in a natural leaf-mold soil, reach a height of twenty feet or more. At the peak of the blooming season in late winter and early spring the Los Angeles Camellia Council holds its annual Camellia Festival, which is one of the best attended events of the year.

A crystal-clear stream, descending from a spring in the hills two miles away, flows swiftly over its rocky bed in the camellia forest. Deeper into the woods, nature trails wind among oaks and giant redwoods, sycamores, ginkgos and tall pine trees to a pond where ducks, geese, green herons, killdeer, belted kingfishers and even an occasional great blue or black-crowned night heron may be seen. At the Bird Observation Station, hummingbirds, grosbeaks, robins, finches, sparrows and sometimes hawks may be seen at close range. Owls, turkey vultures and a variety of migrants also visit the Gardens regularly.

The History of The Rose Garden, so popular since the Gardens opened that it had to be moved to a more prominent location, has some 350 types of historic bloom in chronological order and is still one of Descanso's main attractions. Unique in the annals of American gardening, it includes examples of such important historical varieties as *Rosa damascena,* the Damask rose. With its beautiful carmine-red blooms, it is known as the rose of romance and poetry, and is thought to be a native of Syria imported into France and England by the Crusaders. Another *R. damascena* variety stands with the *Rosa alba* in the History of The Rose Garden as a symbol of the War of the Roses, the famous thirty-year battle between the British Houses of Lancaster and York.

The *R. centifolia,* known commonly as the Cabbage rose, is a reminder of the romance between Mark Antony and Cleopatra. It is said that Cleopatra, in captivating the venerable warrior, covered the floor of her banquet hall and ballroom with the petals of this lovely flower.

Near the History of The Rose Garden is the Garden of Modern Roses containing the finest All-America Rose Selections beginning with The Chief, Apricot Queen, California, World's Fair and Dickson's Red selections for 1940. On the opposite side of the History of the Rose circle, the Sun Garden features irises and

Photos: John Howell

Gottscho-Schleisner, Inc.

Opposite: The teahouse at the Oriental
Pavilion in this garden landscaped by
Japanese-Americans is popular with visitors.

Above: Of the Gardens' 165 acres, 30 of the
most centrally located are devoted to shade-
loving plants such as azaleas and rhododendron.

287

Above: The Gardens' thousands of camellias
are shaded from the hot West Coast sun
by ancient California oaks.

John Howell

chrysanthemums along with choice examples of native flora.

Across from here is a Garden of California Native Plants containing cactus, manzanita, yucca, ceanothus, and many interesting succulents. According to the Gardens' director, Mark J. Anthony, a former nurseryman who sold Manchester Boddy his first camellias, the purpose of this garden is to show Californians what can be accomplished with their magnificent heritage of native plants. Interest in this garden has increased since recent forest fires have created a hazard to homes in the chaparral-covered hills of southern California. A primary purpose of Descanso Gardens, Mr. Anthony notes, is to show people how to bring beauty to their own gardens. A Saturday morning demonstration of rose pruning, for example, may bring a thousand home gardeners to Descanso.

All roads in the garden lead eventually to the Hospitality House, the pillared, white Boddy mansion which, in addition to being a meeting place for local garden organizations and a gallery for monthly art displays, is headquarters for the Gardens' educational center. Several adult education courses are taught here, mostly for the home gardener, but also for the professional. The youth education program includes workshops and field trips for youngsters from the area's schools.

One popular project, mostly for children, is the annual celebration of Arbor Day, March 7, to commemorate the birthday of Luther Burbank and National Conservation Week. Every child who visits the Gardens' on this day receives a seedling tree to take home.

The Gardens are now a popular and publicly supported attraction in the Los Angeles area, but the Descanso Gardens Guild continues to give full support in improving them. In 1966 they presented a beautiful $50,000 Oriental Teahouse. The surrounding Japanese Garden, complete with a tranquil pool, was designed in authentic Oriental style by members of the Japanese-American community along with the Descanso Gardens staff. In this lovely setting, under Japanese lanterns, tea and cookies are served in the teahouse daily, except on Monday.

Looking at Descanso Gardens, its beautiful camellia woods, its roses, its cactus and eucalyptus, and the numbers of people who enjoy its benefits, one can fully appreciate the power of a few dedicated individuals to preserve and improve the beauty of our nation. For all that is to be learned here from the horticultural displays this, in the end, may be the greater lesson.

Opposite: As equally attractive as the
colorful Camellia Forests and Rose Garden
is the fern grove with its many green hues.

Koloa, Kauai, Hawaii

PLANTATION GARDEN (MOIR'S)

A *Superlative Collection of Exotic Flowers and Cacti*

Werner Stoy/Camera Hawaii

Aloe vera, one of the healing aloes, was probably used by early missionaries in Texas and Mexico for its medicinal qualities.

Opposite: In this tropical environment, colors develop a richness usually not found in many of the same plants on the mainland.

Along the southern shore of the "Garden Island" of Kauai, Hawaii, at the juncture of Poipu and Spouting Horn Roads, an inconspicuous fork in the road marks the location of Koloa Landing, which 150 years ago was a regular stopping place for the whaling vessels that sailed these seas. It ranked as the third largest port in the islands. Crossing the bridge here and taking the road to the left along the shore and past the salt pans of Poipu, you come to Plantation Garden (formerly Moir's Gardens) which, today, is one of the most beautiful places in this most scenic part of the world.

Here is a superlative collection of exotic flowers, cactus and other succulents, covering some seven acres around the home of Hector Moir, former manager of Koloa Plantation, the first sugar plantation in Hawaii. The Moirs began their garden in 1932, personally collecting and placing the enormous cacti and delicate orchids, and planning the garden's design. The place was named *Pa'u-a-Laka*, meaning "Skirt of Laka," for the ancient goddess of the hula. According to legend, there was once a hula training temple here. Although the public preferred to call it Moir's Gardens, the ancient Hawaiian name fittingly evokes the sensuous and unusual beauty of the tropical planting.

Much of the area is devoted to fine collections of cactus and other succulents. There are hardy desert plants, set among different levels of lichen-covered volcanic rock, and colorful water lilies in the cascading pools. One of the most interesting of the many kinds of cactus to be seen here is the *Cereus*, which often reaches heights of thirty feet. One fine specimen here has grown to a weight estimated at three tons. During the summer and fall the branches are covered with myriad large flowers. Even more outstanding is their fruit, ranging from the size of a hen's egg to that of a large orange or apple, brightly colored in shades of red and yellow. The fruit is much prized by the Indians of South America where the plants grow wild. All of the cacti in this tropical environment develop rich shades of green as compared to the dull color of many plants found on the mainland.

The night-blooming cereus (a term generally applied to the genera *Monvillea, Harrisia, Selinicereus* and *Hylocereus)* display their

Werner Stoy/Camera Hawaii

Above: Mexican Indians tap the maguey plant
and draw off in large gourds a colorless
liquid which, when allowed to ferment,
becomes the drinkable, intoxicating pulque.

Opposite: Seeming to belie the differences
between the desert and tropics, a palm tree and
an agave grow side by side. The agave is
a member of the amaryllis family.

293

Bud Carter

Cacti at Plantation Garden are rich green. They are enhanced by nineteen cascading tropical water lily pools.

Courtesy Plantation Garden, Inc.

large white blooms only after the sun has set, and are a major attraction here.

The term "succulent," deriving from the Latin word, *succulentus,* meaning fleshy or juicy, applies not only to cactus, but to a large number of other desert-growing plants. In addition to the many kinds of cactus, Plantation Garden has the largest collection of "wonder healing" African aloes in the world. These colorful plants are especially desirable for garden decoration since their candle-shaped spikes bloom all winter. From the time of the early Greeks they have been grown for the healing properties of the liquid in their thick leaves. Early missionaries to Mexico and California probably knew of their medicinal qualities because at least one species, *Aloe vera,* became naturalized in the area of several old missions in Mexico, Texas and California. At Plantation Garden the brilliant red, yellow and orange of blooming aloes contrast beautifully with the darker red of volcanic rock and the greens of surrounding succulents. Another well-known succulent found in the Garden is *Euphorbia,* some of which reach a height of thirty feet.

Adjacent to the cactus and succulent garden is a tropical garden, built around a series of inviting water lily pools. Overlooking the intense blue of the Pacific Ocean, this lush planting distills the essence of Hawaiian gardens. The exquisite bloom of the many

Flower-laden plumeria or South Seas frangipani add color of almost every conceivable hue to the Garden's other plants.

Werner Stoy/Camera Hawaii

The blossoms of the *Agave attenuata*, or
maguey plant, look like shepherds' crooks
and grow to heights of twelve feet.

orchids blends with the color of birds-of-paradise, anthuriums, ferns and palm trees. The bromeliads, in great variety and profusion, are another popular attraction of this tropical garden. Varieties of bromeliads, members of the pineapple family, often grow on stalks from two to eight feet tall, carrying flowers of unusual form in blended shades of white, red, pink, blue, green and yellow. Yellow sisal, coral plants, orchid gray ghost plants, paloverde and red starfish grace the dark volcanic rock. Color of almost every conceivable hue is added by over thirty varieties of the flower-laden plumeria or South Seas frangipani.

Not to be overlooked in this colorful garden is the brilliance of the many birds that find food and protection here. Bright against the green of heavy foliage is the scarlet plumage of Kentucky and Brazilian cardinals, the raven-black of mynah birds and the shimmer of the golden plover. Birdsong heard in the background might be that of the aku (night heron), the aeo (Hawaiian stilt), the akekeke (ruddy turnstone), the white eye, rice bird or the good luck symbol of Hawaii, the pueo or Hawaiian owl. Over thirty kinds of birds are seen in the Garden each year, many of them native Hawaiian species which are now in danger of becoming extinct.

Throughout the Garden there are many historical artifacts. In the tropical garden near the water lilies is a huge whaler's trypot, once used on the deck of a whaling ship to boil down the whale meat and extract the lucrative oil. At another spot is an old millstone used by early sugar farmers to extract sugar and syrup from the cane. Throughout the Garden are large rock works used by early-day Hawaiians as cooking places. The fireplaces are constructed of piled rocks, since the lava-hardened earth was too hard to dig out, and built with horseshoe-shaped walls as a barrier against the wind.

In 1968 Mr. and Mrs. Moir decided to lease their estate and retire to Arizona. It was leased to Plantation Garden, Inc., whose president, Robert Lloyd, plans to maintain the Garden in its present form with some additions to the orchids and the collection of Polynesian plants. The presently unused land surrounding the Garden will be reclaimed for the comfort and convenience of guests. The large rambling plantation house, where kittens now play on the sun-swept lawn, will be converted to an inn that will carefully maintain the gracious turn-of-the-century atmosphere. Some Polynesian shops will be added, including one that will specialize in foods produced from plants growing in the Garden.

When they were at home, Hector and Sandi Moir used to take guests on a tour through their garden. Today the tours are conducted by Hawaiian *tutus* (grandmothers) who have a wealth of interesting legends and stories to tell about the Island, as well as specific information about the Garden and the plants.

Botanists who have seen Plantation Garden regard it as one of the best of its type in the world. But whether you are a scientist, a photographer, or simply a lover of nature's beauty, Plantation Garden is surely one of the most lush and colorful displays of tropical flowers and foliage to be found in the United States.

Photos: Bud Carter

The Garden contains many hardy desert plants set among lichen-covered volcanic rock and colorful water lily pools on different levels.

One of the most interesting of the many kinds of cactus at Plantation Garden is the *Cereus*, which often reaches heights of thirty feet.

Werner Stoy/Camera Hawaii

These twelve-foot *Cereus* specimens stand
like sentinels against the sky in
the northwest corner of the Garden.